Quilting Lessons

Quilting

Notes from the Scrap Bag of a Writer and Quilter

Lessons

JANET CATHERINE BERLO

University of Nebraska Press Lincoln & London

Parts of "Sedna, Squared" appeared in " 'Great Woman Down There!':
Northern Perspectives on Female Power and Creativity,"
Nimrod International Journal 8:2 (spring/summer 1995): 30–36.

♾

Library of Congress Cataloging-in-Publication Data

Berlo, Janet Catherine.
Quilting lessons : notes from the scrap bag of a writer
and quilter / Janet Catherine Berlo.
p.   cm.
ISBN 0-8032-1318-2 (cloth : alk. paper)
1. Berlo, Janet Catherine.   2. Quiltmakers—United States—Biography.
3. Women art historians—United States—Biography.   I. Title.
NK9198.B47   A2   2001
746.46′092—dc21
[B]   00-061591

𝒩

To my sisters,

B. J. Berlo and Judith Berlo-Tucker

Contents

Acknowledgments

As always, the sisters come first:

I thank my scribbling sisters, Martha Baker, Vicki Henry, and Elizabeth Ptak, wise writers whose editorial counsel, gentle nagging, and general cheerleading played a big part in this book being published. I thank my biological sisters, B. J. Berlo and Judith Berlo-Tucker, who first dragged me to the fabric store in 1956 and haven't ever let up since, I am glad to say.

To my academic sisters, and sisters of the heart, Aldona Jonaitis and Ruth Phillips, without whom no writing project is possible: Your confidence in my detour from the world of academic writing was more important than you can ever know. I thank my artistic sisters, Kate Anderson and Phyllis Plattner, whose enthusiastic response to this manuscript convinced me it had something to offer to other creative people besides quilters.

I am grateful to my quilt-studies sisters, Patricia Cox Crews and Carolyn Ducey, both of the International Quilt Studies Center at the University of Nebraska, who made me take this manuscript off the shelf and resuscitate it. I am also grateful to the quilters' guilds, academic audiences, and artists' groups to whom I gave readings from 1994 to 1999, for their warm reception of portions of this manuscript.

To Barbara Snider, M.D., whose challenge during my writer's block, "why don't you just sit down on the couch with a pad and paper and see what comes out?" brought forth this manuscript, I offer an especially heartfelt thank you.

As always, the biggest thanks belong to Bradley D. Gale, husband and coconspirator extraordinaire, who now has more quilts (and more quilt fabric) in his house than we can ever use in two lifetimes.

Quilting Lessons

INTRODUCTION
Piecing for Cover

Beth, my research assistant, rockets through the front door in a flurry of enthusiasm.

"I found some biographical information on that Lakota artist! I looked through the census records for 1890, and found her last name."

I try to comprehend what she is saying, but I feel as if I'm struggling to arrive from a great distance. I've spent the last seven hours immersed in patchwork of vermilion and burnt umber. I find it hard to speak. Even more frightening, I find it hard to comprehend the words that tumble out of Beth's mouth.

"Then I searched the biographical directory of Native artists, but that was a dead end. And then I went back to the records of the Indians who went to the mission school . . . "

I interrupt her. "Is it all written down in your notes?"

"Yes, but . . . "

"Good," I manage to say firmly and, I hope, at least a little gracefully. "Thanks for all your hard work. I'll read it later. I'm in the middle of something else right now." I hustle her out the door.

As soon as the door closes behind her, I begin to cry. Not big sobs.

Just soundless tears, seeping from beneath my closed eyelids. I stalk into the living room and huddle miserably on the couch.

"My academic life is over," I think to myself savagely. "I can't even understand simple sentences anymore. She might as well have been speaking Chinese. I just knew I had to get her out of here." I knock the pile of photocopies and typed notes off the coffee table and onto the floor, and kick at it ineffectually.

Fleeing the mess of papers, I climb the oak staircase of my hundred-year-old Victorian house in St. Louis, bypassing the second floor, on up the carpeted stair to the third floor, my aerie, my safe haven. It used to be my study. But gradually, over the past few months, the desk and writing table have grown dusty and lifeless, while the other side of the room has been transformed into a quilt studio.

Here my stacks of fabric comfort me. Sorted and piled according to color, they await my touch to animate them, turn them into the controlled chaos of what I call my "Serendipity Quilts." Here the only language is color and pattern.

It is January 1993. I am in the sixth month of my quilting depression. Nothing makes sense to me but the rhythmic buzz of my sewing machine, the hiss of the steam iron, and the riotous hues that surround me.

My husband leaves for work at 7:45 A.M. I don't answer the phone or the doorbell. My job is all-day, intensive color and pattern therapy. I am piecing for cover. I am quilting to save my life.

The word "depression" evokes a picture of extreme lassitude: unwashed hair, unmade bed, physical stasis. My depression wasn't like that. It involved a total shut-down of my normal daily life as a prolific historian of American Indian art and the unfurling of a new part of me.

Sort of a Dr. Jekyll and Mrs. Patchwork.

While I don't know anything about brain circuitry, the way I've come to explain it to myself is that the verbal, linear pathways in my brain shut down. The parts that were hungry for color and texture took over. Picture the way kudzu takes over roadside ditches in the South or mint colonizes the herb patch. Everything else overgrown, spindly, unreachable.

When I wasn't quilting, I wasn't alive. On most days, I felt that I literally needed those vibrant hues in order to breathe.

Some days my brain craved blue. From my large stash of fabrics, I would pull a selection, spread them out in varying combinations, and form a pleasing palette for my day's work. Teal and midnight blue patterns, cobalt stripes, a sprigged hyacinth. Black with jagged ultramarine swirls. I would arrange them next to each other, add two, subtract one. When I had a group of seven or eight that looked right, I would begin to cut and piece. I seldom had a prearranged plan in mind. My body craved the colors and the kinetic act of cutting and piecing, cutting and piecing.

To an old-time quilt maker, the notion of "piecing for cover" implies making something serviceable for everyday use, as distinct from a wedding quilt or the one put out for a special houseguest. But to me, "piecing for cover" describes what I did during the eighteen months of my depression. I see a vivid image of myself sheltered under a big quilt or surrounded by swaths of fabric, hiding within their protective coloration. I hear "piecing for cover" as a phrase akin to "run for cover" or "take cover." It evokes quilt making as an activity that protected and camouflaged me during a time that, in retrospect, can only be described as a breakdown of all "normal" systems.

It happened suddenly, in the middle of the summer of 1992. One week I was laboring over the last third of a book I was writing on American Indian women's art. The next week I was paralyzed. All writers and scholars experience this occasionally. To pass the time, we read novels, weed the garden, bake cookies. A few hours or a few days later, the work resumes. Or we sit at the desk, sharpen pencils, take notes, shuffle index cards. In fits and starts, we get over the hump, and a paragraph emerges. And then, slowly, another.

But I was in total revolt. I couldn't even walk by the desk, never mind sit down at it. I had read about writer's block, but in the two decades since embarking upon a career as an art historian, it had never happened to me. I didn't really believe in writer's block (the way some women don't believe in menstrual cramps). Then suddenly I was doubled over, my insides all blocked up.

I had been working on the book sporadically for five years. I completed several other major projects during that time, but this was the special one, the one that was going to be different from my previous academic works. I called the book-in-progress "Dreaming of Double Woman: Reflections on the Female Artist in the Native New World." The cover design juxtaposed two images: a nineteenth-century black-and-white photo of a Plains Indian woman seated on the ground, bent over her beadwork, and a colorful late-twentieth-century painting by Laurie Houseman-Whitehawk, a Winnebago artist from Nebraska. In the painting, a hip, modern Plains woman in traditional powwow dress, wearing Ray-Ban sunglasses, stands with her hand on her hip, looking directly out at the viewer. The book is about historical Indian art as well as contemporary artists in bead, fiber, clay, and paint. It critiques the traditional stereotype of the Indian woman as drudge.

I've worked in many different parts of indigenous America for the last two decades, from Guatemala to the Canadian Arctic, and I wanted this book to be a strong, vibrant synthesis of my own and others' research, with a feminist spin. In the realm of art, for centuries Native women have combined their interests in bold graphic design, complex technology, science, philosophy, religion, and community. The book was more than two-thirds finished. Why had I suddenly fallen mute?

Like the visual arts in Native American communities, quilt making is still central to many American women's lives (be they Anglo-, Afro-, Native, or any other qualifier) at the end of the twentieth century. We don't need to do it "for cover" in the practical sense any more, for there are plenty of inexpensive blankets simply to keep us warm. Today it provides a different sort of cover—a space in women's lives. For some, it is time out from the heavy responsibilities of raising children and running a household. The full-time child psychologist, educator, cook, referee, and family economist needs an oasis. Many homemakers find that oasis in making quilts.

Other women need an oasis from the arduous demands of professions where we travel to distant cities, write books, report on the news, order pharmaceuticals, or vote on bills in the state legislature.

In either case, we come to quilt making looking for a respite from one set of challenges by embracing a very different set—involving color, pattern, sensuality, skill, and order, in an ever-changing mixture.

I had sewn, sporadically, since childhood, had even made a quilt or two. But what possessed me, that July afternoon, to drive out to a fabric store and drop six hundred dollars on a Bernina (the Mercedes of the sewing machine world) and begin to cut and piece? It was an unexplained craving, like an anemic craving apricots, kale, or steak for the iron. Some part of my psyche knew what it needed. The scholar-me was just along for the ride.

The piecing and quilt making continued from summer into fall. I mastered Log Cabin, Card Tricks, Churn Dash, School House, Bear Paw, and many other patterns whose names evoke vivid images in the minds of quilters. By Christmas I had transformed my large study— the entire top floor of my Victorian house—from a scholar's retreat to a space divided equally between writing and sewing.

The two halves have an uneasy alliance, however, mirroring the warring factions in my psyche. Two of the three long trestle tables that for years had held photos, Xeroxes, notes, articles, and books-in-progress now hold fabric, patterns, transparent rulers, graph paper, and pins. A tabletop placed on two forty-inch bookcases forms a tall cutting surface that allows me to stand and work without straining my back. Beneath the table are bins of cotton fabric, sorted by color. "My stash," as we quilters call it.

New track lighting illuminates the side of the long, rectangular room devoted to quilting. Meanwhile, the other half of the room sits in shadow. Stacks of books and photocopies and file folders of notes untouched in months serve as a rebuke to the past fifteen years of my life as a scholar and professor. I struggle with how to reconcile these two parts of me into a coherent whole.

In the past, I have found the writing of a book to be relentlessly linear, doggedly logical. Building a scaffold of argument based on the foundation of other people's prior investigations. Meticulous library research. Endless pedantic footnotes, proving that one has examined all previous arguments and either incorporated or refuted them. It's an exhausting and lonely business.

In my quilt making, I scorned precision, pattern, and measurement. I craved the playful, the provisional. I needed freewheeling and accidental. I worked intuitively, no rules, starting with recognizable nuggets of pattern, and then exploding them, encircling them, fragmenting them.

I settled upon the term "Serendipity Quilts" for the work I was doing. I looked up *serendipity* in the dictionary: "an apparent aptitude for making fortunate discoveries accidentally."

Every day I worked silently, as if in a trance. No talk or music in the studio. All the noise was visual, the action vigorous and energetic. It entailed constant movement from cutting table, to sewing machine, to floor, to ironing board. Each piece placed was improvisational, rapid. I wanted it to grow organically, without benefit of too much rationality, order, or predictability.

For the first big Serendipity Quilt, I choose greens and blue greens. Craving these colors, I bought more every time I went to the fabric store. I didn't know why these were the visual imperatives. Now, as I write, I hear the voice of my teacher, Robert Farris Thompson, twenty years ago, in a graduate seminar at Yale on African art and philosophy. One day he gave an extemporaneous oration on blue and green. It went something like this: "Blue and green: very soothing colors to the Yoruba people. Cooling colors, the colors of ocean water and river water, where powerful goddesses live. The color of cooling leaves from the deep forest. The color of fresh palm fronds. People need to be soothed, have their minds assuaged with the powers of blue and green."

Was I soaking myself in blue green, cooling the restless irritation that filled me? Some days I couldn't get enough. These colors saturated me. I imbibed them through my eyes and my fingertips.

Serendipity Quilts are like the therapy sessions I embarked upon seven months into Quilt Madness. Rationality, planning, order, and control are not successful strategies in therapy. Opening yourself to experiencing what's on your mind is. In Serendipity Quilts, as well as in therapy, surprising connections are made. Extraordinary patterns emerge. It's important to trust that a larger pattern is being formed. It takes a while to see it.

It was mute, kinetic activity in a field of color and pattern. I was reprogramming my brain. Debugging. Brainwashing.

It must have worked. When I sat down to work on my Native American art history book after nine months of quilting, the title and outline for this memoir, Quilting Lessons, came out of my pen instead. Different neural patterns had been formed, new pathways forged.

Toward the end of Quilt Madness, I published an essay in Piecework magazine, only the second nonacademic publication of my life. Called "Loss," it was about my resolution to find a path through sorrow by making a mourning quilt, should my husband die before me. I evidently touched a nerve, for some extraordinary letters were forwarded to me from the magazine, messages from women who had lost their mates. In the face of their real grief, I felt humbled, almost embarrassed, by how glib my words about an imagined grief seemed when set against the naked sorrow in the lives of others.

The losses these women described were not always from death. One wrote about the dissolving of an engagement and her turning to quilting as a solace in her grief over a marriage that was not to be. As a neonatal nurse, she now runs quilt-making workshops for parents who have lost their newborn babies. All the participants piece for cover, for comfort from their grief. As she did with her broken engagement, they must come to terms with a life that is not to be.

Another woman wrote, heartbreakingly and at great length, about the loss that she says is worse than the loss of a mate through death: the loss of a functioning partner whose body lives on after a massively debilitating stroke. In the year that she has sat at his bedside, she has pieced for cover, as she railed against the universe for the loss of this vital man. Any more words from me would have been sorely inadequate in the face of her enormous rage and sorrow. But I sent some fabric, to aid in her enterprise—a mute but tender act of support for her loss.

A third woman wrote about the pain of a double loss. For when she lost her husband to cancer, she lost her ability to quilt as well. Quilting was so closely linked with the domestic tranquillity and joy of their evenings together that to quilt just redoubled her grief.

So many stories are sheltered beneath these pieced coverlets.

As a country, we're engaged in a great national act of piecing for cover—the AIDS quilt. The memorial panels, each three feet by six feet in size, are pieced, appliquéd, painted, collaged, glued—all manner of media and methods of forming them. At the end of 1987, the AIDS quilt had nearly two thousand panels. Today, more than twenty thousand have been contributed to this national quilt of mourning. How many football fields does it cover now? Enough to shelter us all?

The panels of the AIDS quilt commemorate thousands of vibrant people whose lives were cut short. They also document the love and pain of those left behind. *Common Threads*, the film made in 1989 about the AIDS quilt, documents the lives of some of the dead and their survivors. It shows Tracey Torrey making a panel for his lover, David Campbell, who has died; shortly thereafter, diagnosed with AIDS himself, Torrey cuts and paints his own panel, carefully filling in the letters of his name and the military title that clearly was so central to his identity. This moment in the film touched me like no other. This was, to me, the last word in "piecing for cover"—Naval Commander T. E. Torrey creating his own emblematic shroud, memorial, talisman, and monument. His oasis, his lone island, in an enormous international archipelago of loss.

Compared to these huge, irretrievable losses, my loss was decidedly minor: I didn't lose a life or a mate; I just temporarily lost my way as a writer and an academic. But by "piecing for cover," I discovered what was fundamental.

The act of making patchwork quilts provided an oasis of grace in my life. I pitched my pieced tent in that oasis, finding shelter and warmth for my psyche. During those eighteen months, my oasis grew larger than the terrain around it, as I compulsively filled twelve- or fourteen-hour days with cutting and stitching.

I repeat: I was piecing for cover. I was quilting to save my life.

I have long operated on the principle that I don't know what I think until I see what comes out of my pen. As a teenager and young woman, what came out were poems, short stories, and lengthy journal entries. Since my early twenties it has been a master's thesis, doctoral dissertation, several dozen articles, and a number of books.

But when, for almost a year, nothing came out of my pen, I was stymied. Eleven months were almost exclusively nonverbal and non-linear, filled with color. Yet they also were filled with confusion over the loss of my scholarly work. For during the months that the quilter emerged, the scholar disappeared. From being a productive writer and researcher I was transformed—seemingly overnight—into someone who lives and breathes for patchwork.

Yet of course it was NOT overnight. Increasingly I see that I am picking up pieces of my past. Not only the intellectual work, like creative writing and art making, that I so avidly pursued in my youth, but also the work of understanding my place in the world, including the small world of my nuclear family: my cold, standoffish relationship to my mother, my close yet distant bonds with my older sisters.

I am an art historian, trained in pre-Columbian art and archaeology. For more than a decade I have specialized in American Indian art history, focused increasingly on women's arts, such as Navajo rugs, Lakota beadwork, and Maya textiles. So turning to quilt making is not as jarring a transformation, perhaps, as if I had been a molecular biologist turned quilt maker. My two sisters also happen to be quilters.

It is probably not insignificant that this was the year I turned forty, traditionally a time of change and reevaluation, a time of turning to more primal, elemental themes of one's life. I had been subliminally dissatisfied with my academic work for a long time. In *Dreaming of Double Woman*, I was trying to move away from arcane, scholarly studies to a book that would have relevance both to a wider audience and to me as a woman. Writing about archaeological topics was intellectually challenging during my twenties and early thirties, but it had little meaning in my daily life. When an article was written and sent out to make its way into the world of academic discourse, it no longer meant anything to me personally.

And now I was stalled. In free fall. Needing to integrate more parts of myself into my work, to stitch all of these pieces into a meaningful whole, I turned to quilt making. This is a record of that patchwork in progress.

Loss

L ike all women, I worry about loss. Specifically, the loss of my husband. While we don't have a traditional, old-fashioned marriage (I am not financially dependent on him, and we have no children), he is my best friend, my coconspirator. We are both loners. We joke about that: a pair of loners.

Sometimes when he is out longer than I expect or there is a violent thunderstorm during rush hour, I worry that he is dead. While I recognize that this fear is irrational, I also know from talking with other women that it is not uncommon. Women who have children experience these terrors far more often in regard to their children, I suppose. But all my terrors are focused on the loss of one man. I believe that without him I could not breathe.

It frightens me to think of this loss. I worry that I would not survive it. I know from the way I have handled other losses in the past that it is easy for me to lose my bearings. In the face of grief I have experienced crippling anxiety and depression. But for this worst of all possible losses I have a survival plan.

Looking at my quilt books some months ago, I was moved to tears by a quilt made in 1839 by Elizabeth Roseberry Mitchell of Kentucky.[1]

It is a repeating Lemoyne Star pattern, but it has a central square that is a graveyard with a gate. A path leads into the graveyard from one side of the quilt. In a corner of the central square four cloth caskets are appliquéd in a cluster, each labeled with a name. Two of Elizabeth Mitchell's sons died in the decade before she made this quilt; two of the caskets bear their names. Other caskets make up an intermittent border on three sides of the quilt, waiting to join those already inside the graveyard. The border of the quilt is a picket fence. The quilt is pieced in browns and beiges, but the pieced stars are vibrant despite their somber tones. They perform a muted dance of hope across the surface of the quilt. This coverlet shows a great deal of wear; did its maker shroud herself in it for many years after her losses?

If my mate should die before me, I will make a mourning quilt. Like Elizabeth Mitchell's quilt, mine will be elaborate and detailed, not one that can be completed in a week or a month. Intricate in pattern and execution, it will be composed of many small pieces to which I must pay close attention as I work. Not being a member of an organized religion, I will have no conventional rituals of mourning to follow. This will be my path out of sorrow.

Will I choose the traditional colors of mourning? I don't know. I like black and use it a lot in my quilts. But Bradley likes yellow. He introduced me to the possibilities of yellow, a color I had long scorned. Perhaps his quilt will explore all its permutations. I should add more yellows to my stash, just in case.

In their oral history of elderly quilters from Texas and New Mexico, The Quilters: Women and Domestic Art, Patricia Cooper and Norma Buford record one widow's reminiscence: "Mr. Thompson and I, we worked side by side all them years. Up till I was sixty-five. He taught me everything I know about building and carpentry. We was more than married; we was partners. When he died, we was in the middle of building this house for ourselves, and after the funeral I come home and put on my overalls and finished this house in thirty days. I never looked up till I was through. I lost fifty-seven pounds during that time. Then I took up quilting."[2] Quirl Thompson Havenhill found useful ways to clear a path through grief. Quilting is my contingency plan for finding my way through sorrow. Other women have grappled with loss in other ways, but a common thread emerges: Our work will help us survive.

It's not surprising that I'm focused on loss right now. My work and Bradley often seem to be the only two things I need in the world. Both have been easy, steady, and rewarding relationships, until the recent fickle desertion of my work. I have always defined myself in relation to my work; having lost this primary relationship, it makes sense that I should worry about the health of the other.

Clearly, my psyche is making backup plans. Oddly enough, it's not seeking solace in friends or family but in a new kind of work, based in color and texture and pattern.

JULY 1993
Unfinished Business

I have been experimenting with the breaking of boundaries, the transformation of patterns, the dynamic play of asymmetry, and the fracturing and spiraling outward of patterns. Not only in the act of quilt making but in the very patterns I have chosen—or rather the very patterns that have seized me and compelled me to experiment with them—I have been signaling change, transformation, the rupture of predictable pattern on a grand scale.

Sounds like my life at forty.

Today I sat down, resolving to work on my book on Native women and art, which I have neglected for almost a year. I told myself that I would not censor or edit as I wrote. I would simply accept what came forth, without worrying about precisely how it would fit into the book manuscript. What came pouring out was the introduction and framework for this book. I quickly made a list of possible topics for small essays. The first on the list of my topics was "Loss." I promptly scribbled the first draft of the previous essay.

The author of eight previous scholarly tomes, I have been intending for my current project to be different from my other academic writings. Freer, more experimental, more self-revelatory. It is having a difficult and painful gestation. Yet, instead of writing about other women's art, I find I am making my own. It speaks of dizzying color, patterns transformed, new freewheeling forms. I have been acting out with fabric what I need to do in my life.

I telephone Kate Anderson, a St. Louis artist I have known for years. We are not close friends, but when we talk, we are always on the same wavelength.

"Kate, do you think of your art making as play?" I ask her without preamble. I think I know what the answer will be and prepare to settle in for a satisfying discussion of playfulness in our work.

"No, it's not play," she says adamantly, surprising me. "I have another friend who's always exclaiming 'Oh, I envy you! You must have so much fun in your studio!' It drives me nuts."

"If it's not play, what is it?" I ask.

"It's passion," she declares. "It's physically arduous, but soothing too. I think that people call it 'play' because they only know how to talk about it in childlike terms. They don't have a vocabulary for adult passion for work. But when I'm in the studio, I feel like I tap into an elemental part of myself. I enter another zone. It's almost meditative."

"I know exactly what you mean," I tell her. "I feel that too."

Neither of us is religious, nor are we New-Agey, so we know what we don't mean by this vocabulary, which skirts dangerous territory.

"It only takes a few minutes of working with the fabric and I'm there," I begin.

"Yes!" she interrupts. "It's in the touch. I connect instantaneously. As soon as I touch my materials, I begin to feel soothed."

"What about the design process?" I ask her. "Isn't that like play?"

Kate and her husband collaborate on big painted constructions. Combining driftwood and colored wooden elements, the works look like three-dimensional wooden quilts. There are always lots of unfinished pieces strewn about the Andersons' studio. I have observed them sitting in their easy chairs, in front of their work-in-progress. Coffee cups in hand, they have endless, subtle discussions about shade and pattern, rhythm and repetition.

"Well, we experiment with the placement of forms. There's a lot of moving pieces around like jigsaw puzzles . . . I guess it is play!"

Kate chuckles, seeming startled at this insight. "Oh, my God! It's a whole series of unfinished jigsaw puzzles we're playing with!"

I too play with my puzzle pieces of soft fabric spread out on the carpet. Working hard at this play, I have been teaching myself to make a way to the next part of my life, to break out of the predictable and tired patterns of the past. I have leapt readily into the nonverbal, nonlinear, kinetic world of quilt making, for it has nourished some part of me that was starving. Yet now, in these pages, I am moved to articulate how that process has been transforming my life.

The quilt maker inside emerged when I was in rebellion against the small, loud, controlling part of me who demanded that I finish an unfinished book. In the twelve months since then, I have completed seven large quilts and have made another dozen small pieced projects like table runners and place mats.

The book's hulking presence rebukes me every day. In addition to the unfinished book, I have a half-dozen pieced quilt tops that I have not sandwiched and finished up, and many pieced squares that will make their way into another half-dozen quilts.

Eventually.

When the time is right.

As all quilt makers know, piecing and quilting is a great unfinished business.

In my unfinished book on Native American women's arts, one of the chapters I did complete concerns the insights that myth offers concerning the role of the Indian woman as artist. The Lakota and the Iroquois, for example, have legends in which a spirit woman doing weaving or quillwork is hampered from finishing her work. Yet this is a good thing, according to these stories. For if such women finish their work, the world will come to an end. These Native American stories express a glorious version of the maxim "women's work is never done." But how wonderful that the work in question is not cooking, cleaning, or child care! It is art making.

I like it: Women's unfinished arts allow for the continuation of life as we know it.

Many quilters know for a fact that the world will come to an end before they manage to complete all their half-done projects. An informal poll of my two older sisters reveals that Judith has six quilts and four other projects unfinished. B. J. has twelve unfinished projects, as well as a backlog of two dozen more that have been started only in her imagination. She also has the world's largest fabric stash. Like the Sioux woman of legend, she could sit and quilt until the end of the world without using it all up.

B. J. talks about the comfort of having more than enough fabric.

"I know I'll never be bored. And if I'm snowed in during a New Hampshire blizzard, I'm not trapped."

I think that for many quilters, my sister included, who may not have richness, extravagance, and abundance in other aspects of their lives, there is something deeply satisfying about this sort of "material" abundance and the many unfinished projects that go along with it.

Old quilt squares, those small fragments of the past, are oddly moving. They are remnants of other women's hopes and aspirations, glimpses of the colors and patterns that inspired gluttony and hope, a link with our female ancestors. Judging by the number to be had at flea markets and quilt fairs, it is clear that this unfinished business has been going on for a long time.

Last fall I took a class on finishing techniques at In Stitches, my favorite St. Louis quilt shop. Ellen, our teacher, encouraged us to buy a large box of five gross stainless-steel safety pins. I did an approximate computation in my head and then spoke out loud.

"Five times 144?" I asked, puzzled. "That's over 700 pins! Why in the world would I need over 700 pins?"

"It's 720 pins," Ellen said firmly. "And be sure they are stainless. You don't want rust on your quilt."

"How would the quilt get rusty in the time between sandwiching the layers and quilting the top?" another student asked.

Ellen laughed. "You'd be surprised. You put it aside for a few weeks. And then you start another quilt. Or maybe family life takes over your time. Sometimes the quilt will sit for a few months—or even a few years—before you get the opportunity to quilt it."

A mere three months into Quilt Madness, I laughed at the thought that I would ever have more than one or two unfinished quilts. I bought a small box of pins, and then another, and another. Six weeks later I bought two more. Now I am ready for that damn box of 720 pins.

Why is unfinished business okay in quilting but not in writing?

I was hosting one of my favorite scholarly sisters, Diane Bell, who had come to my university to give a lecture on Aboriginal Australian women's life and art.[3] As we sat in my back yard, drinking tea, I complained to her about my languishing book.

"It's just such a loud rebuke in my head, Diane. All I hear is 'Unfinished!' 'Unfinished!' It's driving me crazy!"

"Don't let it do that. I began a book in the 1970s. It didn't want to be finished either. I put it aside. Wrote three other books, I did," she tells me matter-of-factly in her broad Australian accent.

"That book didn't want to be finished then. It took almost twenty years of working on other things before that manuscript wanted to be finished.

"And I matured so much as a scholar in those years," she confides, brushing her wild mane of gray-brown hair back from her face. "When I picked it up again, I framed the discussion much more intelligently than I would have two decades before."

I have to have faith that what I have put down will be picked up again. As I brood about my unfinished book, I take solace in the fact that sometimes pieced work is long in the making. Every quilt book I look at and every quilt show I attend lately gives me solace in this regard.

Nebraska quilt maker Juliamae Duerfeldt started an appliquéd gladiola quilt in 1946. Forty-two years later, in 1988, she finished it.[4] Genevieve Zurn pieced a Grandmother's Flower Garden Quilt top composed of over two thousand hexagons when she was a nine-year-old girl, in 1928. She quilted it in 1975.[5] New York needle artist Edith Almann started a Yo-Yo Quilt in 1934 at the age of seven. She finished it in 1987, at sixty-one. It has 5,856 little gathered yo-yos in it, so perhaps she can be forgiven.[6]

But can I be?

I abandoned my book at a time when it seemed like it had at least that many disparate facts, subtopics, and intellectual threads hanging from it. I had thoroughly researched what had been written in one hundred years worth of the anthropological literature on Native American women. I had wrestled with theoretical and methodological writings that had arisen from the feminist reexamination of women's lives over the last four decades, as well as the postmodern critiques of anthropology, feminism, colonialism, and art. I had interviewed contemporary artists and worked in Native communities. Why was I suddenly paralyzed?

Perhaps I should pack it away, like an unfinished quilt, secure in the knowledge that the time will come to finally piece it together.

Standing in front of an appliquéd Flower Garden Quilt at a Kansas City quilt show last week, I was eavesdropping on two older spectators.

The elegant silver-haired one turned to her sidekick and said in exasperation, "You know, I really must finish my Flower Garden Quilt some time. I started the blasted thing in 1939!"

Her friend gave a knowing nod.

AUGUST 1993
Writer's Block

W hen I began this book, I played with the idea of titling some of the essays with the names of quilt blocks: Delectable Mountains, Robbing Peter to Pay Paul, Nine Patch. But since I was intending to write about the creative process in general and my own writing problems in particular, I knew that not all the essays would be so titled. After all, I wanted to write about writer's block. I typed the title Writer's Block on the computer screen and then began to laugh.

Writer's Block as a quilt square!

What would Writer's Block look like in the Crazy Quilt of my life?

Is it just a blank muslin square? After all, Writer's Block is the absence of words, ideas, marks on the page. But it is certainly not a blank square in my case! For me, Writer's Block has been the most complex, convoluted square of all. Perhaps it is one of the twenty-two-inch blocks that comprise the huge green Serendipity Quilt that I made this past winter for my own bedroom. Writer's Block is absence of words, but fullness of fabric and color and pattern. Asymmetry. Nonlinearity. All the things my lopsided, rational, linear brain had been denied the past few years.

For the first months of my quilt-making apprenticeship, I worked relentlessly, putting in much longer hours than I ever had on my academic work. I was aware of a great hunger for vivid color, for the pleasing interplay of patterns. I didn't always make finished quilts. Sometimes I just experimented: a block of Bear's Paw pattern in reds and rich navy blues; three blocks of Courthouse Steps in blacks and vibrant purples.

Later I became more reflective about the process. Clearly I was teaching myself a new way of working. Ten months of my own daily quilting lessons made it possible for me to view the rest of my life in better perspective. What exactly are the preliminary quilting lessons of my apprenticeship?

Try to care less about the finished product and have more enjoyment of the process. In writing, all too often the writer is consumed with the idea of the finished product: the book, the poem, the article in an academic journal. In quilting, we find the finished product beautiful, and we may take great pride in our achievements, but we only do it because we enjoy the process. No one who doesn't enjoy cutting up fabric into little pieces and sewing them back together again has ever been successful at making pieced quilts!

It is crucial to accept the messiness of the process. At my writing desk, I always harbor the illusion that if only I could clear out the disorder, I could more easily work on the book. As a result, I often spend the two or three most productive hours of my morning answering letters, filing the endless stack of photocopies that threaten to take over, or reading just one more article. And so I squander my precious energy, trying to "get to" the work instead of just *doing* it.

In my quilt studio, I always have three or four projects in active production. (This doesn't include those that are half cut out or half pieced and put away for a few months.) The window seat might be piled high with the yardage and scraps of the Navajo Star Map Quilt that I've been laying out. The reds, blacks, and whites lie there intertwined. Next to them are the color choices I am mulling over for Diane Bell's place mats: It might take a few days of passing by the stack to determine if those colors are electric enough to shine in the same room with that vibrant woman. On the cutting table is a basket of two-inch strips from the green Log Cabins I've been making. Coiled in the corner by the iron is the binding for yet another project. Yet when I come to the cutting board in the morning and prepare to work, I don't feel the need to organize, or clear out, or clean up. As long as there is space enough to measure and cut, I simply begin work, amid the festive disorder.

If one road is blocked, try another. I am just in the beginning stages of trying a new way of working on my book. Since the old way of sitting at a desk and working at a computer for five to seven hours a day no longer works, I am trying a more patchwork approach. I take small pieces of it with me, so that I can integrate a half-hour's worth of writing into the living room, especially when the afternoon sun is shining through the back window. I am trying to write spontaneously rather than to rely so much on the framework of the scholarly literature, the footnote, the quotation. This is more like a Serendipity Quilt than a measured, patterned square.

If a subsection of a chapter is not unfolding logically, I lay the pages out on the floor, in the same area where I lay out quilts in process. It works equally well for the mapping out of complex ideas. The overall design will often emerge. Paragraphs and pages can be shifted around, cut up and pasted, until they look right.

Be patient until the right path emerges. When I begin work on a new quilt, I feel a great sense of excitement and experimentation. First, I choose the fabric. This is a long process, and one I carry around in my head and in my purse. Some of the fabrics will come from my stash. Little strips of these chosen fabrics pinned to a file card lurk at the bottom of my large shoulder bag, in case I find myself in the vicinity of a fabric store.

When I have assembled an ample range of fabrics, I make a few practice blocks. Sometimes it is clear right away that a certain pattern or a certain conjunction of fabrics will not work for the idea I have in mind. It would never occur to me (or to any other quilter, I hope) to throw away those trial blocks or to be angry that they didn't come out right the first time. I put them aside for later use. These blocks may prove to be the inspiration for another quilt next week or next year, or one of them may become the center portion of a pillow for a quick gift.

Why then am I so pragmatic and stingy about my writing? If the ideas won't flow, I get angry. If my mind is sluggish and won't produce complex thought, I castigate myself. I panic, grow melodramatic: I will NEVER write again!

In contrast, as a quilter, I know that there are days to begin a complex Pineapple patch and then there are days to do simple rotary cutting of strips for a Log Cabin Quilt. Both are satisfying. Each has its own rhythms. And some days, of course, all one can do is get in the car and drive to the fabric store. In that safe haven, one can walk down the aisles in a daze, imbibing color and pattern. Looking for something to jump-start the brain. Sometimes all it takes is a fat quarter-yard of the right Nancy Crow fabric.

Postscript

In the final stages of preparing this manuscript, I discovered that there is, in fact, a pattern called Writer's Block. Judy Martin illustrates it in her *Ultimate Book of Quilt Block Patterns*.[7] It is not a pattern I would intuitively have chosen to depict my malady. But the more I looked at it, the more it fit.

Martin illustrates a pinwheel in gray stripes against a black eight-pointed star. When I began to picture the pinwheel endlessly spinning in the breeze, it seemed an increasingly appropriate pattern. That's how the scholarly lobe of my brain has felt these last few months: containing only a rickety plastic pinwheel, spinning aimlessly, powering nothing and going nowhere.

SEPTEMBER 1 9 9 3
In My Sisters' Studios

B oth my sisters have been quilting for over a decade. Now, more than ever, I regret the thousand miles that separate their households from my own. Judith is ten years older than I, B. J. four years older than Judith. B. J. has always been my teacher, the one I looked up to. She departed for art school, and her adult life, by the time I was four, so an idealized relationship was easy; we had very little experience of the customary frictions of sisters growing up in close proximity.

Judith and I had a more normal, messier sisterhood. She recalls what an annoyance I was at seven while she was trying to impress her teenaged boyfriends. I, in turn, carry memories of small acts of impatience on her part, during those years when we lived in the same household and she was often responsible for looking after me. But now we aren't seven and seventeen; we are forty and fifty.

And for the first time, she is my teacher. In my family, I have long held the role of the precocious one. With the exception of the art lessons that were my legacy from B. J., within the family I have mostly been self-taught, a bit aloof. Starting in my teenaged years, my modus operandi was to find my own way and report my successes back to my family. (In a family where I am the only one who finished college, these successes must seem a bit mysterious: Ph.D. at twenty-seven and the incessant writing of books and giving of lectures.)

I cut and piece, alone in my own study, no special St. Louis friend to share my successes and trials with. One thousand miles away, Judith too works alone in her studio in Kittery Point, Maine. But she works amid a quilting network that stretches across New England and across North America because of the guilds she belongs to, the workshops she has taught, and the classes she takes every summer at "Quilting by the Lake" in Cazenovia, New York. (We have always referred to these summer seminars of hers as "going to quilt camp.")

Last January I went to New England to visit my sisters. It was not the usual hectic dash across the landscape to see friends in New Haven and Newton, parents in Boston, and sisters in New Hampshire and Maine. Instead, I flew into the Manchester, New Hampshire, airport where B. J. works. I spent two days with her, on a grand tour of the fabric shops of New Hampshire and Maine. Then I spent two days in Judith's quilt studio in Kittery. She rents "office space" in a quiet professional building a mile from her home, working there most days, undisturbed by the household telephone or the rebuke of laundry that needs folding. She has only her music tapes, her big work tables, her shelves full of fabric, and the power of her own creativity.

Though I had been to Judith's studio before, this was the first time I appraised it with the eye of a quilt maker. I appreciated the height of her spacious worktable. I noticed that her shelves of fabric were covered to avoid fading by the natural light that streams in through her traditional New England six-over-nine windows.

I was expecting that Judith and I would work in her studio side by side, as companions. I carried with me a half-done project that I intended to complete. Instead, Judith began to show me things. Before long, without any formal planning, I was the student in a full-fledged all-day seminar: How to Sew Perfect Pineapple Blocks Using Paper Templates. Neophyte quilters eagerly pay fifty dollars apiece to attend a group class like this. I had my own expert private tutor!

All day Judith was at my beck and call. For the first time, I came to appreciate deeply her painstaking perfectionism. She taught me to clip threads closely after each bout at the sewing machine to avoid a nasty tangle. She suggested trimming away the dark seam allowance behind a light fabric so that its shadow would not mute the crisp color effect.

I admired some of her hand-dyed fabrics, and she gave me a piece of the most beautiful one. She let me root in her scrap boxes (sorted by color, as only the most meticulous artist will take the time to do!) and take some green prints that I admired. When I exclaimed over two different Pineapple blocks she had made, Judith offered them to me. They were left over from two big commissions she had done. I incorporated them, as well as the scraps, into a huge green Serendipity Quilt I made for my bedroom. It seemed necessary that pieces by each sister be included in one of my first major undertakings, as if I were part of some larger, genetic imperative.

Taking up quilting in my thirty-ninth year has given me a new level of rapport with both of my sisters. While I will not soon be their equals in terms of technical excellence, in a larger sense my sisters and I meet as peers in this arena, as we have nowhere else.

I'm not the baby sister tagging along to the fabric store. Nor am I the college professor who moves in an academic world unfamiliar to them. We are artists working together. We are laughing women.

We are sisters.

My oldest sister, B. J., approaches her textile work quite differently from Judith. She has a quilt studio in her home, which is crammed full of fabric, patterns, and half-finished projects. But she is, single-handedly, a traveling quilt studio. Having worked for a major airline for more than twenty-five years, she has access to almost unlimited free travel passes. So she travels to visit her best friend in Pennsylvania or me in St. Louis about as casually as most of us embark upon a trip across town.

During the many years when I was not actively making art, I looked forward to seeing what projects she would bring with her: crocheted afghans, knitted sweaters, hand piecing for a commissioned baby quilt. I got my first look at the Olfa Rotary Cutting system that has revolutionized modern piecework when B. J. whipped a green rubber mat and a funny little yellow pizza cutter out of her big canvas bag on one of her frequent trips to St. Louis.

B. J. goes to visit her best friend, Paulette, (the fourth Berlo sister, she quips) in Erie, Pennsylvania, with the following projects for a five-day visit: fabric for two Trip Around the World Quilts to cut out; three pieced quilt tops that need to be sandwiched and basted; two purchased patterns that she might be in the mood to buy fabric for. She and Paulette quilt and laugh all day and evening, every day, and most of the projects get done.

Winter 1992: B. J. flies out to visit me in Los Angeles while I am a visiting professor at UCLA. As a present she brings me a small Olfa mat and rotary cutter and gives me lessons in speed cutting. Of course we have to go out and buy fabric in order to have the lesson, but she has come equipped with the name and address of one of the most famous shops in the country: Mary Ellen Hopkins's Crazy Ladies and Friends in Santa Monica. We eat the legendary Oreo cookies that are bestowed upon each new visitor to the shop. Then we each buy about one hundred dollars worth of fabric. For her, this is reasonable. She sews all the time. I, on the other hand, am camping out in an apartment that is already too small for my husband, my bloodhound, my computer, and me. I have no sewing machine in California. Moreover, I have not sewed much in the last ten years. This is utter madness! But I was seduced by the sheer possibilities: all those colors and patterns!

I'm not sure why B. J. knew that I was almost ready for a mat and cutter. Six months later when my scholarly batteries ran down and the quilt-making engine inside me came roaring to life, the tools and fabric were there waiting for me. Now how did she know that I would need these things just a few months hence? Sister's intuition is a mysterious business.

B. J. reports her pleasure at the phone messages that I have left on her machine over the past few months:

"Hi! I am reporting that I have finally succumbed to sisterly peer pressure—I bought a Bernina today!"

"Hi, Beej! I made my first Bear's Paw today! Do you know there are thirty-two little triangles in just one Bear's Paw!"

"Beejerooni—can you get vacation days in the middle of June? There is a big, new quilt extravaganza in Kansas City, and I am going to drive out and see it. Can you come?"

"Would you look through your fabric stash for chocolatey browns and bring me some when you come next week?"

"Sister! I am in need of some emergency hand quilting lessons. Please come for a quick overnight and teach me!"

B. J., the Flying Quilt Master, can set up shop in five minutes flat. Sometimes she even travels with her Bernina sewing machine. She whips out her tools, her Ziploc bags of diamonds for her Lone Star Quilt in progress (diamonds she probably cut in the last hour before catching a plane somewhere), and wherever she has alighted becomes a quilt studio. In her work habits, B. J. reminds me of the Maya weavers I studied in Guatemala a decade ago. Those frugal women fashion a back-strap loom from a few pieces of wood, string, and warp thread. Because the tension on the loom is produced by means of a strap that hooks around her own back and a line that can be tied to any post or tree, a Maya woman can weave anywhere; she just rolls up the loom, batten safely secured inside, and goes. Have loom, will travel!

Many modern quilters say that the reason they like to do hand piecing is that they always have something small to work on, no matter where they may be. B. J. does hand piecing of course, and this goes in her capacious bag too, but she doesn't stop there. Any and all projects are portable for the Flying Quilt Master. I picture her now, flying through the air, not on a U.S. Air 737 nor on a magic carpet. It strikes me now just how fitting it is that her favorite quilt pattern is called Trip around the World.

See her now, zooming across the sky!

SEPTEMBER 1993
Tall Girls' Tales

B y the age of four, I recall tagging along with B. J. and Judith on trips to the fabric store. While they studied patterns and yardage requirements, I marched through aisles of fabric, hands held out to either side, feeling the bolts of material: the coarse, scratchy wools in all their dark hues; the shiny silks and satins; the prim cottons. I am convinced that this was one of my formative experiences. As an adult, studying and collecting Maya textiles in Guatemala, I experienced that same tactile satisfaction as I examined coarse wool serapes from Momostenango, gauzy silk brocades from Quezaltenango, and austere cotton brocades from Alotenango.

B. J. taught me many things, especially in the realm of women's arts—sewing, knitting, embroidery—but the best lesson was one imprinted on me very early: B. J. taught me to be tall. Despite her best example, though, I suffered a bit in my early adolescence from too-tall-itis.

I recall how we fidgeted in the basement auditorium of St. Joseph's church that hot June day of 1966, sixty-five boys and girls who were waiting to march upstairs to graduate from grammar school. I was thirteen and only two inches shy of my final height of five feet eleven and three-quarters inches, which I achieved the following year. In a processional symmetry that delighted the nuns, but that five eighth-grade girls experienced as the most excruciating public torture, we were lined up by height.

"Why couldn't I be one of the anonymous ones," I thought to myself resentfully, "safe in the middle of the line?"

I was last. Everyone would be looking at me, sticking out there at the end. Taller than everyone. Beanpole. Giraffe. Stretch.

Katherine Ronin, Mary Murphy, Patty Duffy, and Barbara Morrissey shared with me the indignity of marching behind the tallest boy, (a mere five feet six or so). But make no mistake about it—only one of us was last.

We had been practicing this processional for a week, so I was well rehearsed in its humiliations. But today was the day that hundreds of parents, thousands of brothers and sisters, cousins and aunts, everybody in the world, in fact, would take note of the fact that I was the tallest eighth-grader in the universe.

At least my white A-line dress with bell sleeves was more elegant than the babyish pastel jobs most of the other girls wore. My mother and I had bought it in the Juniors' Department at Filene's. (My elongated body was way beyond the seven-to-fourteen size range of the Girls' Department.) Of course, the sleeves did only come three-quarters of the way down my arms, my long, bony wrists and big hands jutting out from their lace-trimmed ends.

Because it was more important to show that you were grown up than to worry about whether you were adding another half-inch to your height, I did wear the "squash heels" that were fashionable that year. They provided only the smallest elevation, but proved that the wearer had moved beyond the girlish realm of "flats."

My thirteenth year was the only one of my long, tall life in which

I recall a misery in proportion to my height. It had to do with a brief intersection in which all the boys were small and my own self-consciousness was very large indeed. While I had always been taller than all the other children, I had usually perceived this as an asset. At camp, I was accepted by the older kids, whom I idolized. Adults often let me hang around to overhear grown-up conversations, because I didn't seem kiddish. At eleven, I listened with rapt attention as B. J. and her friend Alice exchanged gruesome medical stories. No one tried to shoo me away. After all, I was nearly eight inches taller than twenty-seven-year-old Alice—so how young could I be?

B. J. was telling Alice about the delivery of her baby, through an early type of natural childbirth combined with hypnosis.

"So the doctor comes in and he says, 'Relax your muscles, B. J.,' which is the hypnotic phrase we've been practicing for weeks, and suddenly I don't care that my cervix is almost fully dilated and that I feel like I'm about to shit a basketball."

My six-feet-tall father and my five-feet-two mother inexplicably produced three tall daughters. (But Judith, the middle daughter—and at five feet seven the shortest one—is not tall enough for this tale.) For more than four decades, my oldest sister, who is a shade over six feet, and I, the baby, a shade under six feet have been the two closest family members, though fourteen years separate us.

Those fourteen years are crucial ones. B. J., born in 1939, came of age in the 1950s. Her offbeat elegance was wasted on that decade, when Doris Day and Sandra Dee were the templates for young womanhood. Though not a beatnik, she did appropriate some of the funkiness of the beatnik aesthetic into her personal style. She dyed her hair red and wore thick eyeliner. Her clothes, most of which she made herself, accentuated her willowy frame.

As a child of the '60s, I had an easier time of it. The cultural mores had relaxed considerably and, more importantly for me, my passage was smoother than hers because I always was able to trail in B. J.'s wake.

One of my earliest memories takes place at the New Hampshire seashore. I am three and am sitting where the hot sand meets the icy New

England surf. Surrounded by my red plastic pail, yellow shovel, and a host of other plastic cups and containers, I am busily constructing my sandcastle.

As I focus on some particularly difficult aspect of its architecture, I don't notice that the outgoing tide has captured my pail. When I look up, it is bobbing away. It looks to me to be very far away indeed. I begin to go after it but am frightened by the swirly waves. As I stand there and wail, B. J. strides past me, her long legs cutting through the water. I don't think she even got her bathing suit wet. In a half-dozen strides, she retrieved the pail, turned back, tucked me under her arm, and settled us down to build that castle.

I still remember the look of those long, powerful legs: they got the job done.

When I was six, B. J. was an art student, living in an apartment in Boston. Occasionally my parents would allow me to spend the weekend with her. These are the happiest memories of my early childhood. She bought me real artist's materials—pastels and charcoal. We worked side by side.

B. J. had a Greek boyfriend, a graduate student at Harvard, who took us out for ice-cream cones and chop suey. Greg Spiropolous called her "Bijou" instead of B. J.

With the pedantic demeanor I had even as a child, I patiently corrected him. "No, Greg, her name is B. J.—it's two letters. She doesn't like the name Bette Jane, so you have to call her B. J."

My sister laughed, and gently corrected me. "*Bijou* is a French word, Janet. It means gift or jewel. It's a special nickname Greg has for me."

I watched them whisper together as we strode across Boston Common toward the Swan Boats in the lake. Greg bought me a small, stuffed hound dog. At night, after I was supposed to be asleep, I spied on them through the glass doors that separated B. J.'s bedroom from her living room. They kissed and slow danced to Johnny Mathis.

Greg was five feet seven. His cheek rested on her chest.

I thought they looked swell.

A decade later, as a junior in high school, I met my first lover. Carl Gustafson, a Swede, was just a bit over five feet seven as well. Impervious to the chortles of the small-minded, we reveled in each other's minds and bodies, which to us were perfectly matched.

All through my childhood, as I grew and grew, aunts would say approvingly, "Oh, you'll be nice and tall, just like B. J." But by thirteen, none of that mattered anymore. I was marooned in my misery. And my beloved B. J. was not in the church pews to cheer me on at graduation; she was two states away, marooned in her own hectic life, managing her one- and three-year-old boys.

I was on my own.

And yet, to the credit of tall girls everywhere, I didn't slouch. I was savvy enough to realize that that only made you look like a tall girl who slouched, not a less tall girl.

A few weeks before that mortifying graduation, I had endured another searing humiliation, but of a less public sort. Sister Virgilia had decided that we must practice our public speaking. So each student in our eighth-grade class had to stand at the front of the room and give a two-minute speech.

What was worse (and here we see the clueless innocence that only a nun could muster), all of the other students would critique this speech—not through publicly offered commentary but through personal notes, which would be collected and passed to the speaker to read in private.

Thirty years later, these are the only notes I remember:

"Hey, Stretch! How's the weather up there?"

"How do you like playing basketball with the Boston Celtics, Stretch?"

"You're a monster, Stretch!"

Obviously, the boys had a firmly established nickname for me. This was the first I'd heard of it.

Stretch! My face burned, and my shoulders flinched. I felt as if I had been scalded. My eyes brimmed with tears. As the next person spoke, I looked around the room (from my vantage point in the last row, of course). Who could have written such mean things?

Not Kevin O'Donnell, I hoped. It had only been three years since he'd asked me to marry him! (We were closer in height then.)

It had better not be Robert Rotundi, with his completely apt surname. He had no grounds to criticize my appearance!

Probably one of them was from Billy Burns, class clown and all-around juvenile delinquent. He was always getting into trouble with the nuns. Wait till I tell Sister Virgilia about this! (But of course, I wouldn't. I may have been an A student and a beanpole, but I was not a goody-goody.)

We only did this nasty public-speaking exercise once. Perhaps Sister Virgilia did retrieve the crumpled-up notes from the wastebasket.

I walked home alone that day, replaying my humiliation. I imagined the boys snickering as they folded up the notes, then assuming their altar-boy smiles as Sister Virgilia collected them.

It was all so perplexing. Most of the time, I was proud to be tall. I felt powerful, sophisticated, older. With B. J., I always felt glamorous. We shopped at the Tall Girl Shop in downtown Boston. We bought elegant fabric together and planned sophisticated outfits.

When I was alone, navigating the Boston subway system, my art materials tucked under my arm, on my way to the Museum of Fine Arts to draw the Egyptian sculptures or the Greek portrait heads, I would pretend to be a college girl, an art major. I would scrutinize the short kids on the subway car.

"Short, all of them short," I'd tell myself disdainfully. "They look like they are only twelve or thirteen." I, of course, looked older. And that is the essential longing at that age—to be older.

It was only in that eighth-grade classroom that I felt like Alice, who had sipped from the bottle marked "Drink Me" and grown till her head hit the ceiling and her arms stretched out the doors. There, I was constantly, shamefully, aware of how much space I took up. My legs poked out into the aisle from under my too-small desk. A good two inches of wrist jutted out of my ever-too-short sleeves. The waist of the jumper of my brown school uniform rode way too high on my long torso.

Why were the rest of them so short? And why did my height annoy them so much?

"Don't they know that tall girls wear clothes better?" I told myself savagely, repeating what my mother and sisters had said so often. I kicked a rock all the way down Orchard Street, studying the ground. "Don't they know tall girls grow up to be models?"

"There aren't any midgets in *Seventeen* magazine," I said to myself loftily and loped the rest of the way home.

At the time, my own humiliation was so all-encompassing that it never occurred to me that others might have endured worse than to be called "Stretch." With hindsight, I can only imagine the bodily critiques inflicted on the other tall girls that day. Poor Barbara Morrissey was not only tall, but was saddled with the formidably large breasts she had acquired in sixth grade. What unspeakable things did the boys write to her? And Mary Murphy, with her thick waist, ruddy complexion, and hacked-off, dun-colored hair—with six older brothers as her only role models, she acted like a stevedore-in-training. Did thirteen-year-old boys use epithets like "lezbo" and "dyke" back in 1966? How early they learned that they were entitled to comment on female bodies!

The blinding misery of being the tallest girl in eighth grade soon abated. But for all of us, these preadolescent humiliations are seared deep into the psyche. Recently, when I recounted to B. J. the tale of my eighth-grade graduation, she told me that she had spent the second semester of her senior year in Catholic high school brooding about the fact that she was sure to be last in the graduation line. But miracles do happen (especially in Catholic school), and three boys shot up quickly in the last weeks of the term. B. J. still remembers the names of the three growing boys who protected her from end-of-the-line ignominy. My sister thanks you, Frank Barba, Ray Camigliano, and Pat Donelan.

The cosmopolitan public junior high where I attended ninth grade harbored a few girls as tall as I, and, God be praised, one even taller! She was a patrician WASP, smart and sardonic. The first time we saw each other, in the hall, between classes, we both nodded. An acknowledgment of a sister in the Tribe of Tall.

That same year, British model Jean Shrimpton took the world by storm. She was my height, which imbued me with a certain stature in the eyes of my ninth-grade peers. I scrutinized her photos and avidly read her vital statistics in *Mademoiselle*: height—5 feet 10 inches, weight—125 lbs., favorite color: purple.

Same as me! Same as me!

I gained even more currency that winter when the expensive British outfit I had cajoled my mother into buying for me (with endless promises of how many kitchen floors I would wash and how many Venetian blinds I would vacuum) was featured in *Seventeen* magazine *after* I acquired it. There was a purple mini-skirted, form-fitting jumper, a lime green turtleneck to wear under it, a purple-and-green checked jacket and matching bell-bottom pants. I saved up my babysitting money to buy the perfect pair of purple Capezio shoes (size ten by now) to match.

In just one year, I had grown into my body. "You should be a model!" my new friends would exclaim. "Those clothes look fantastic on you!"

I realize, in retrospect, that B. J.'s interest in sewing and in elegant clothing, passed on to me, helped save us from dissatisfaction with our too-tall female selves. This was one of the few gifts our neurotic and difficult mother did give us. She was interested in clothes and wished she could have worn all those stylish and dramatic things that were not appropriate for her chunky five-feet-two frame. And so she was pleased to buy them for us, within her limited finances.

I have a photo of B. J., one I've kept in my own stash, away from the family archives, since I was small. It was taken in 1961 at a family party celebrating her engagement. In her high heels, she is as tall as her fiancé. She wears a white skirt and a black sheath blouse with only one shoulder. Her hair is short, dyed a reddish hue. She wears big earrings and eyeliner. She looks cosmopolitan and elegant—not at all like a too-tall girl from a small Massachusetts town.

In 1989, I eloped with my Bradley. Until I had the photos developed, I was unaware of something I had done: in my short hair (dyed red), my big earrings, and my black-and-white fitted dress with only one shoulder, I too look elegant, and perfectly at ease next to my shorter husband.

Now, when my husband (five-nine) says, "Hey, Stretch! Can you reach that flour canister on the top shelf for me?" I smile and slam-dunk it into his hands.

SEPTEMBER 1993
The Family Scrap Bag

W riting these essays has caused me to reach deep into the scrap bag of memory, as I concoct this literary crazy quilt.

Clearly, B. J. is a vivid part of my most joyous childhood memories. I regret that I have no recollection—and no photo either—of the matching felt poodle skirts that B. J. sewed for herself and for me in 1955, for her high school fashion show. Apparently I stole the show with my sweet little skirt and the ruffled underpants I flashed at the audience. This incident looms large in my sister's mental scrap bag, as does the time I spilled chocolate milk on the white dress she had just finished sewing for the junior-senior prom. I'm told I'm lucky to be alive.

My mother is not a gardener, so it surprises me that one of my earliest and happiest memories involving her is of planting pansy seeds along the side fence in my early-childhood home on Summer Street in Fitchburg, Massachusetts. When I worked with deep, rich purple fabrics for a quilt for my friend Kate Kane this past winter, I saw those deep, velvety petals of the pansies of my childhood.

And so memory and action interlock and carry me forward: I planted pansies this season because of the purple fabric in my studio. Then I saw some marvelous pansy fabric in a local fabric store. I bought a fat quarter to make a pieced mat for my mother's table. We are not emotionally close; this is my distant, abstract way of honoring her.

My mother, Jeannette, was a modern young woman in the 1930s. Not for her the somber, heavy woods of her mother's house or the old-fashioned task of making quilts. She filled her first home with blond Heywood Wakefield furniture in streamlined style. Her mother, Delvina Clementine Tousignant, did make and give her a quilt for an engagement present in 1934. As was common that decade, it is an appliquéd quilt, of tulips on a muslin background.

Although it graced B. J.'s bed in her preteen years, that quilt later became mine. My last memory of it is in my previous house, the one I shared with my former husband. The quilt got lost in some move between St. Louis, Washington DC, Providence, and St. Louis, again, in my peripatetic 1980s. It wasn't fancy or unusual. In fact, it was rather homely. But I wish I still had that loving product of my grandmother's hands. I'm jealous when I meet women who tell me they possess quilts from four generations of women in their families.

Our mother is pleased at her daughters' quilt making, for she sees it as a link to her mother, and her mother's sister, our great-aunt Georgie, who was our mother's confidante. I remember an elderly, half-blind Aunt Georgie, who was an excellent cook, but B. J.'s earliest sewing memories are of Aunt Georgie helping her to make doll clothes in 1945.

"I would cut a long piece of thread from the spool. My idea was that the longer the thread, the fewer times I'd have to rethread the needle," B. J. remembers.

"Aunt Georgie told me in no uncertain terms that it definitely was not ladylike to be raising my hand holding the needle up in the air as high as that little arm would go. She told me to cut my thread twelve inches long."

My own early-childhood sewing memories involve Aunt Caroline, my father's sister, who was accomplished at all the needle arts. I still remember the amusement and stifled impatience on Aunt Caroline's no-nonsense Bostonian face when I—like B. J., seven years old—chided her for not tying both ends of her thread into a knot before sewing. I even undertook to show her how they must be firmly tied. I was certain that she would not be able to sew anything securely with that one loose thread flapping in the breeze!

Aunt Caroline was my father's oldest sister. In his own laconic way, he describes a relationship that is clearly like my oldest sister's relationship to me. Caroline was his special friend and champion in a noisy household where the youngest, quietest child was sometimes overlooked. She also watched out for him in his early adulthood, during the Depression years, when she fed home-cooked meals to a young working man with little money. For this, she is also special to me.

When I was a child, my father and I would drive to see Aunt Caroline once or twice a month. I had my father to myself during the thirty-five-minute ride to her house. I don't know why my mother or my sister Judith did not go on these jaunts, but Daddy and I went alone. At Aunt Caroline's we usually had some tasty home-baked treat, and often I was given a needlework project to do as we sat quietly in the living room while they talked.

Aunt Caroline died when I was in my teens. I think of her when I thread my needles (usually knotting just the one thread, Aunt Caroline!) and when I bake her special blueberry muffins.

Bradley usually creams the margarine and sugar for me. And we have this exchange, which has become formulaic. Its familiar, teasing intimacy pleases us both.

"And what shall we have on Aunt Carolyn's blueberry muffins? Orange marmalade?" Bradley asks, trying to say "aunt" like a Bostonian, but getting the broad, flat vowels wrong, as Midwesterners always do when they try to mimic us. It comes out sounding like "unt."

"It's pronounced Caro-LINE," I tell him fondly. "AUNT Caro-LINE. Now pipe down and add the blueberries." ("Pipe down" is my father's voice, mildly telling us incessantly giggling ten-year-olds nothing more than a mild-mannered "pipe down," no matter how annoying we were.)

Caroline Berlo Koch's Blueberry Muffins
(adapted for a more health-conscious era)

½ cup margarine
¾ cup white sugar
2 eggs
½ teaspoon salt
2 scant teaspoons baking powder
½ cup low-fat milk
2 cups blueberries (preferably small, tart ones;
    frozen ones will do in the winter)

1 ½ cups white flour
½ cup whole-wheat flour
a dash of cinnamon

Preheat oven to 375°F.
Cream the margarine and the sugar. Add eggs, cinnamon, salt, flours, baking powder, and milk. (Do not overmix or muffins will be tough.) Fold in the blueberries.

Grease a muffin tin with margarine, making sure to cover the top surface of the pan as well as the cups. (This is so the crowns of the muffins don't stick.) Pile the mixture high in each cup. Sprinkle the tops with a mixture of cinnamon and sugar.

Bake for 25–30 minutes, until the tops are browned and the muffins look done. Cool in the pan for a few minutes, then thump the muffin tin down hard on a table surface to dislodge the muffins.

This recipe makes 10–12 muffins.

Recipes in a quilter's diary? It's decidedly part of the aesthetic, one of the scraps that goes into the work as a whole. Recipes are central to women's culture, as are diaries, quilts, and other forms of needle arts. The feminist artist Miriam Schapiro has called this whole aesthetic bundle "femmage," a female play on the word "collage."[8]

Woman cannot live by fabric alone. Once in a while food is necessary.

SEPTEMBER 1993
Navajo Star Map

S tars are my favorite shape for piecing. Not the big Lone Star composed of hundreds of tiny diamonds, which thrills so many quilters, but small, repeating stars. Among the first quilting patterns I experimented with was "A Star for All Seasons" by Wendy Gilbert.[9] I made several table runners and place mats and then began to innovate with this basic pattern. I enlarged the star and scaled it down. I discovered a way to cut strips of complementary fabrics so that I could make stars that looked harmonious, although each was slightly different. For my best friends, Aldona and Ruth, I made lap quilts composed of stars of different colors and varied borders. Next I worked with the star from Jean Wells's Milky Way Quilt pattern.[10] After making a quilt with this repeating pattern of dark and light interlocking stars, I played with color variation in individual stars.

I was hooked.

Last May in San Francisco, I had a wonderful conversation about work and quilts and life's multitude of choices, with my friend and colleague Margot Blum Schevill. Having been a professional opera singer, a voice teacher, a weaver, a museum curator, and an anthropologist, she understands the pull between the world of ideas and the world of the arts. She advised me on my writing problems, exclaimed over my snapshots of my quilts (for by then I had begun to carry a small book of them, like snapshots of children, less to show off to others than to show myself when I was feeling worthless for the barrenness of my writing life). Margot commissioned a quilt from me.

"Deep reds and black and whites," she told me, "so that it can go in the bedroom with my textile by Hopi weaver Ramona Sakiestewa."

Flipping through my book of snapshots, she exclaimed "I like your asymmetrical, dynamic quilts best."

So I began to make stars in reds, blacks, and whites. Large ones and small ones. I encircled some with Pineapple pattern, others in Log Cabin. As I worked with the colors I had chosen, they began to evoke Navajo rugs—the deep, saturated red known as "Ganado red" for the famous trading post in Ganado, Arizona, where so many Navajo women bought their dyes and sold their rugs; and the natural, undyed off-whites, blacks, and charcoals seen in modern Ganado rugs. Navajo women weave splendid textiles that collectors the world over seek out and Mexican weavers copy. Some Navajo rugs have visual affinities with historic American quilts, no doubt because trader's wives made quilts during those long winters on the reservation. The weaver, like the quilter, plays with repetitive patterning, drawing from a large repertory of geometric themes. Yet no two rugs are alike. A weaver's own vision, skill, scale, and color choice make each textile unique.

Navajo weavers have been making rugs (and before that, blankets) for sale and trade for over two hundred years. Yet the commercialization of the art form has not altered the fact that to the weaver the most important thing is the ACT of weaving. It is the process, not the final product, which embodies the deep, underlying principle of Navajo philosophy: the idea that each person bears the responsibility of creating hozho (beauty, harmony) in the world.

The name for my quilt came to me fully formed, halfway through the process of composing the blocks into a pleasing but freewheeling whole: Navajo Star Map. I was puzzled by this name that appeared, unbidden, in my head. I hadn't named any of my previous quilts, although I had nicknamed a certain class of my quilts "Serendipity Quilts." I've read a lot about the Navajo, but I don't recall ever having read anything about Navajo star lore. I called it a star map, but I wasn't really talking about astronomy. Only now, as I write, do I know what I meant by that name. This cloth construction of shooting stars was a map for me out of my impasse. A diagram of the way I had been seized by quilt making and shaken until the pieces of my life reformed themselves in an unpredictable pattern.

I began working on it in June, the same week that I opened for the first time in almost eleven months the thick binder that holds my book manuscript. Halfway through the making of this quilt, I embarked upon Quilting Lessons too. The physical act of making it was a healing act. Just as the Navajo weavers say, creating palpable objects of beauty is healing and restorative for the artist.

This is also the first quilt I submitted to a juried art show. It was accepted for the multimedia show of thirty-six regional artists titled Pieced Works sponsored by the St. Louis Women's Caucus for Art in September 1993. As I was making the quilt, I knew that I needed to document the creative process. I had taken photos of my other quilts when they were finished, but for this one I shot slides of the entire process. I put my best camera, the one I use for museum photography and fieldwork, on a table in my studio and shot a few slides each day as the quilt changed and grew.

This quilt documents a journey out of chaos and into creativity, into the integration of art making AND writing, and even writing about my own art making.

So you see, Margot, I can't give this quilt to you. I need to keep the map for the next time I make the journey.

OCTOBER 1993
Kevin Eckstrom's Chocolate-Raspberry Quilt

'm just finishing a quilted wall hanging made in memory of a friend. As I cut and pieced and machine-stitched, thoughts of him were locked into every stitch. I met Kevin Eckstrom in 1980, during my second summer in St. Louis. He was new at the St. Louis Art Museum, and I attended his first lecture there, on American quilts. He was emphatically enthusiastic about the visionary women of the nineteenth and early twentieth centuries who had made quilts. He presented them in his lecture as artists on a par with the great male painters.

I needed to know this man.

About twenty-three, Kevin was boyish and slim, handsome yet scholarly looking, vivacious yet reserved. He was accomplished in many arenas and well read. I loved these traits about him. A serious pianist, his bachelor of fine arts degree was in music, his master's degree in art history.

Kevin and I became confidants for just a few months, in one of those dizzying, new and heady friendships in which you can't believe how much you have in common. Then we drifted apart, seeing each other just occasionally. Lunch, or working on a video together for the museum, or Kevin dog-sitting at my house became the extent of our relationship. We went on this way for almost a dozen years, sometimes not touching base for six or eight months. Yet we always picked up our friendship easily, talking about art and literature and art-world politics. As I progressed in my career, Kevin occasionally came to me for guidance about his. I wrote many letters of recommendation for him: for jobs, for graduate programs, for fellowships, and for more jobs.

During the years that he worked at the St. Louis Art Museum, Kevin was a jack-of-all-trades: he gave lectures, did research, ran the media center, made educational videos. He curated an exhibit of women's art at my university's gallery and subsequently managed a gallery elsewhere in St. Louis. He always championed the work of women artists.

In the late 1980s, he worked toward his doctorate in comparative literature at Washington University, easily mastering the foreign languages needed for such an arduous course of study. While he was back at school, I was chair of my department and was pleased to offer him occasional part-time work teaching introductory art history courses. He was a gifted teacher; his deeply felt devotion to art and literature were obvious to the students.

Having made the choice to work in nonprofit institutions and later to enroll full time in a Ph.D. program, Kevin was chronically short of funds. Yet he had a great sense of style and always made the best of it. A few years ago, while living in a tiny studio apartment, Kevin wanted to reciprocate for several dinner invitations. He asked if he could borrow my large turn-of-the-century house for a dessert party.

"A dessert party?" I asked skeptically, picturing my house overrun by reveling strangers.

"All you and Bradley have to do is set the table for five; I'll invite one other couple and handle the rest," Kevin assured me.

Intrigued, I agreed. On the designated day, Kevin arrived by taxi, carrying shopping bags full of food and champagne in one hand and holding aloft a platter bearing a marvelous chocolate-raspberry torte. It was a memorable, and for me effortless, party: fine conversation, lots of laughter, even more champagne, and several rich pastries. Kevin had baked a huge tray of rich madeleines. How fitting for a doctoral candidate in French literature to bake the buttery shell-shaped cookies immortalized by Marcel Proust!

But my most vivid memory of that night was the torte. Heavy and dense chocolate, flavored with raspberry liqueur and jam, and crowned with fresh raspberries, it was a sublime marriage of two of the world's most delectable flavors. I asked Kevin for the recipe, and in the mail I got a large white index card, covered with his small, elegant script.

Kevin left St. Louis shortly after that to take a job as a staff writer at the Detroit Institute of Art, a position for which I had recommended him. Only a few months later I got an unexpected phone call from him, telling me that he was leaving Detroit for yet another job, this time at a contemporary art center outside of New York City. As always, he was not too self-revealing. I didn't know if the Detroit job hadn't lived up to his expectations, or if he had a lover in New York. He was, however, full of enthusiasm for the next job, the next new town to conquer, the next opportunity.

We chatted for only a few minutes. I was puzzled at the vehemence with which he said to me, "I hope you know you have been very important to me. You are one of my heroines. I hope you know I respect you so much. I have always looked up to you, and your support has meant so much to me."

Of course, I was touched to hear it. But I didn't know that that he was saying good-bye.

Only a couple months later, I got a typewritten note from his boss at the art center in New York, telling me that Kevin had just died of AIDS, that he had spoken of me often, and that she was sure I would want to know of his death. I cried for days over Kevin, all out of proportion to the size of our friendship.

I was particularly sad that he had kept his illness secret from me. He was always very matter-of-fact about being gay. (In fact, our running joke was how hard it was, for each of us, to find a good man. Kevin had been particularly approving of the good man I finally married.) Kevin's silence did not conceal his sexuality; I suspect it concealed his discomfort with the messiness of illness. Not only a very private person, he was a particularly fastidious one. I assume he didn't want to be fussed over, pitied, or mourned prematurely. As I recalled his phone call to me, I mourned that I did not get the chance to tell him, in turn, how much I valued and respected him and his unique and plentiful talents.

After I began to quilt, I occasionally thought about making a panel for the AIDS quilt in his memory. Yet that impulse didn't feel right, somehow. Such a large, public gesture seemed presumptuous, for my connection to him was delicate and subtle. I chose, instead, to make a more modest wall quilt and donate it to a St. Louis AIDS agency, where it could, perhaps, brighten the day of some other person in pain.

The colors I chose are the ones that evoke my last vivid memory of Kevin Eckstrom, the evening he arrived in a taxi, flushed from too much cooking, yet bearing aloft that perfect chocolate-raspberry confection. The wall hanging is composed of two-inch squares and triangles, in a shape that evokes both a wreath and a cake, with shimmering squares of pinks, violets, and browns, shot through with gold.

It seemed right to make a quilt to honor Kevin; it closed the circle, somehow, for it was a common love of quilts that caused our paths to intersect more than a dozen years ago.

Now dog-eared and chocolate-smeared, the handwritten index card bearing the recipe for Chocolate-Raspberry Torte is the only palpable item I have to remind me of Kevin. Every time I use it, my eyes fill up with tears.

Kevin Eckstrom's Chocolate-Raspberry Torte

1 stick unsalted butter
2 ounces (2 squares) unsweetened chocolate
¾ cup flour
½ teaspoon baking powder
dash of salt
2 eggs
½ cup seedless raspberry jam
½ cup sugar
1 tablespoon Eau-de-Vie Framboise (or other raspberry liqueur)
½ cup chocolate chips
Fresh raspberries and extra jam to garnish the top

Preheat oven to 350°F.
Butter a 9-inch round cake pan and line the bottom with a circle of buttered wax paper.
   Gently melt the unsweetened chocolate and butter together.
   Combine flour, salt, and baking powder in a small bowl.
   Whisk eggs, sugar, jam, and Eau-de-Vie in a large bowl. Add

melted chocolate-butter mixture and whisk till smooth. Whisk in the flour mixture. Add the chocolate chips and stir.

Put mixture into prepared pan. Bake 25–30 minutes. (Center should be moist and edges should not be too dry.)

Cool the cake in the pan for 5 minutes, then invert it onto a plate, and remove waxed paper. Spread a tablespoon of jam over the top surface of the cake while it is still slightly warm but not hot. When cool, add a circle of fresh raspberries around the edge.

Excellent plain or with vanilla ice cream.

NOVEMBER 1993
Simultaneity

Quilts fascinate because they offer so many things to appre-hend at once: tiny quilting stitches creating a rippled, shad-owed effect across the surface; larger pieced areas of repeating pattern and shape; rich layers of color and pattern; successive frames of dif-ferent fabrics chosen as borders. We move back and forth between seeing it all at once and focusing in on the odd geometry of one fabric scrap or the dainty flowers of another.

Some quilts are simultaneously tumbling blocks and steps. They alternately project and recede as the viewer's gaze lingers. Some block patterns can appear to be three or four different blocks, depending on the placement of color and fabric. Judy Martin illustrates this in her book Scraps, Blocks, and Quilts.[11] Thorny Crown looks completely dif-ferent when composed of two fabrics rather than of four. It's hard to believe it's the same pattern. Our eyes adjust, seeing figure and ground differently, depending on changes in color, pattern, and value. Sister's Choice recedes into space if the four corner blocks are a strong color and the background triangles in the other border blocks are quieter. In contrast, this pattern will restrict itself to one planar surface if just two fabrics are used and their values are comparable.

Simultaneity.

In my writing, I am becoming better able to hold multiple ideas, multiple projects in my head at once without fleeing from my desk in dismay. I remind myself that this is genetically hardwired into women, this talent for simultaneity. In the middle of washing dishes, how many of us have turned to the shopping list and added three things to it? While chatting on the phone, we Windex the fingerprints off the kitchen cabinets. While the computer is printing out ten pages of text, there's time to throw a load in the laundry or defrost the leftovers for dinner.

This rule is in effect in the workplace too. My husband and I joke that at the Kinko's Copy Center we always try to be waited on by a female clerk, because she knows how to work on three different orders at once. She will put my request for forty copies of this page in the automatic machine; while the machine runs, she rings up another order. While punching the numbers into the cash register and giving change, she answers the phone. Within the space of ninety seconds, three orders will be done. In contrast, so many of the men working there will follow one order through a linear progression, causing everyone to wait impatiently in line (especially those of us with a double X chromosome, who visualize how easily he could be doing three things at once!).

So far today I have: folded two loads of wash, made six business phone calls, evaluated a manuscript for a publisher, looked up footnotes for an article I am writing, drafted out a complex section of an ambitious quilt I am working on, cut and pieced the background sections of one-quarter of that quilt, and, of course, dreamed about future quilt projects. As I write this, I get up every fifteen minutes to add more ingredients to the stew for tonight's dinner, to stir and taste it, and to set the table. In between times, I write about quilts.

On other days, the proportions of the mix will change; I may spend six hours at the university instead of one and spend one hour at piecing instead of six. But it is important to try (even under the most trying of times) to accept this simultaneity calmly, even when life is threatening to career out of control. It's crucial not to lose sight of one important feature of juggling multiple tasks simultaneously: ensuring a small oasis of pleasure here and there in the day. While the computer prints out a chapter draft or while the wash cycle is on spin, don't forget to take time out to pick sweet peas in the garden. Don't forget to call the friend who has been so sad lately. There might even be enough time to sew the borders on that quilt that is spread out on the work-room floor.

Cultivate it as a particularly female talent, a sisterly pleasure, this juggling act.

DECEMBER 1993
Canyon de Chelly

'm planning a pieced wall hanging to celebrate two things, one transitory, the other of profound duration: a trip made with my two best friends, and the enduring nature of our friendship. Ruth lives in Canada. Aldona, a lifelong New Yorker, now lives in Fairbanks, Alaska. I live in St. Louis. Scholars in the same field, we befriended one another more than ten years ago at a conference. We talk on the phone often. Postcards and photocopied articles fly back and forth across the continent, but we only see each other at academic gatherings or by practicing great sleight of hand with our schedules and travel itineraries.

For the past several years we have established a new tradition: we take an annual trip together. Last year we spent four days at Ruth's lakeside cottage in rural Ontario, reading one another's manuscripts in progress, achieving the proper ratio of low-fat salads for lunch and homemade chocolate torte at 4 P.M., and simply putting things right within our combined worlds by talking endlessly.

The balance we have achieved in our friendship is the balance I'm striving for in my academic and creative life: we move seamlessly from one realm to the next.

"So, Ruth, if you combine chapters 3 and 4, and put that particu-larly elegant part into the introduction, the book will be brilliant," advises Aldona, a superb critical reader, who never loses sight of the big picture.

"And, Ruth, that's 'elegant' with two *es* and an *a*, even though Aldona usually insists on spelling it with three *es*," I can't resist adding, ever the meticulous copyeditor. Besides, Aldona is so much fun to tease.

"You shut up. Maybe you can spell 'elegant,' but can you make an elegant triple chocolate mocha ganache without a recipe?" Aldona, the brilliant pastry chef asks in mock disdain.

"I wouldn't want to," I retort. "Not unless I wore a size six, like you."

"Do you think you could make it for us now, Aldona?" Ruth asks hopefully. Like me, Ruth is five feet eleven and a size fourteen.

This year, because we were all attending a Native American studies conference in Santa Fe, we planned a four-day trip to the Navajo reservation and the ancient archaeological sites within its borders.

These trips are sacred. We make time for them no matter what. Ruth is feeling great pressure to finish her book. Aldona has a demanding job as a museum director. I am teaching full time and had to arrange films and study assignments during my absence. Yet we cleared the slate and reconnoitered on Saturday night in the Albuquerque airport. Sunday morning the expedition began. In four days we drove eleven hundred miles and explored archaeological sites in Arizona, New Mexico, Utah, and Colorado. We dutifully watched the videos in the site museums and bought books and slides to improve our teaching on these topics. We also celebrated my forty-first birthday, read excerpts from this manuscript, and listened to our combined offerings of tapes as we zoomed across some of the most beautiful and desolate landscape that the continent has to offer. The tapes included Patsy Kline (Aldona's choice), Bob Marley and Guys and Dolls (provided and with vocal accompaniment by Ruth), and Kathleen Battle singing Handel operas (my contribution). To us, the wide range of taste exemplified by these selections is a measure of how much our friendship takes in: everything.

Ruth read aloud from Margaret Atwood's most recent collection of stories and from an essay on architecture and astronomy at Chaco Canyon, one of the sites we would visit. I dredged up from memory all that I knew about the ruins and about the Navajo people whose lands we traversed. We discussed work, clothes, our significant others (or lack of them), and every other topic that came to hand. We passed out candy, fat-free cookies, apples, and popcorn as the scenery sped by.

Our particular conversational bone to worry on this day was mothers and daughters. (Aldona and I are just daughters; Ruth is both mother and daughter.)

"So I have a theory to offer about professional women and their mothers," Ruth begins.

"Tell us." She has our rapt attention. This topic is a perennial favorite, a collective sore tooth we are always poking.

"I think most professional women of our generation had mothers who were extremely neurotic and demanding. We didn't want to replicate their stay-at-home lives, so we did everything possible to make our lives different."

We mull this over for a minute.

"It certainly fits my experience," Aldona pronounces.

"Me, too," I say. "I never even liked playing baby dolls as a little girl, because I didn't want to be the mother."

"So what did you play?" Ruth asks.

"Beatnik artist in the studio."

Aldona and Ruth chortle at this.

"I did! My sister B. J. went to art school when I was five, so I knew just how to play it too. I even had all the props."

"But seriously," Ruth persists, "it's because of those neurotic mothers that we are all happy, accomplished women now. The irony!"

"I hope this doesn't mean we have to call our mothers and thank them," I say dubiously. "Talk about a backhanded compliment."

"Oh, yes, I can just hear it now: 'I want to thank you, Ma, for being such a lunatic. If not for you, I'd probably be a housewife trapped at home with three wild teenagers instead of a museum director with a fractious staff of twenty,'" Aldona says, making a face.

The highpoint of the trip was our half-day tour of Canyon de Chelly, a secluded canyon filled with the crumbling ruins and rock art of an ancient Pueblo culture that lived here over eight hundred years ago. For two centuries now, it has been home to some traditional Navajo families and their sheep and horses. The canyon can only be entered in the company of a Navajo guide. Having been elected tour director of this particular trip, I had lined up accommodations and reservations more than a month in advance.

The day dawned flawless, the Southwestern high-desert sky a saturated blue. The air was cold on that Halloween morning, but the sun was warm. Muffled up in blankets and sitting on benches in the back of an open pickup truck, we made our descent into Canyon de Chelly. I had been here fifteen years before, on a blistering summer day, with my first husband, a man who predated these essential friends. I found the Southwest to be a different world in the cool of late autumn, and in their company. They had never been to an archaeological site or a canyon in this part of the world, these women who, between them, have conducted fieldwork in a remote village in Sierra Leone and museum business in a yurt in Mongolia.

Deep in the interior, the sandstone walls of the canyon rose almost a thousand feet, in changing patterns of beige, gold, and brown, depending on the play of sun and shadow. The ghostly ruins rose from the valley floor or from niches in the cliff walls, camouflaged by their similar colors, built as they were out of the rock itself. The cottonwood trees were in various stages of transforming their hues. The heart-shaped leaves ranged from deep green to brilliant orange or gold to dried faded yellow-green, set against bark of deepest brown black. Nearby bushes wore wispy fronds of silvery sage green, which emphasized the vivid oranges and yellows of the cottonwoods even more.

Over the noise of the truck's four-wheel drive grinding over the sandy riverbed, Ruth leaned over and said to me with conviction, "You must make a quilt out of all this."

Yes. A quilt would tell much more than the simple slides I kept shooting, because a quilt could evoke the subtle layers of love and friendship that had brought us there as well.

For over a year I had anguished about my writer's block. My book was at a standstill, the book that had garnered so much praise from my companions at our Ontario retreat some fourteen months before. During that year I had felt paralyzed and disenchanted with my academic work. Yet Ruth had encouraged me to be part of a symposium she had organized the previous spring and lavished compliments on my contribution to it. Aldona had insisted that I submit a paper to the panel she was organizing for a national meeting next February. She simply wouldn't take no for an answer and finally convinced me with indisputably the best reason for my participation: "Janet, you have to be on the panel; that's the only way you can get funding to come to the conference, and that's the only way that the three of us can be together next winter."

In this fashion they pulled me along, and I got over the worst of my alienation from my profession. But at the same time that they encouraged me not to neglect my academic work completely, both Aldona and Ruth were wildly enthusiastic about the world of quilt making I had so thoroughly embraced.

Aldona sent me quilt magazines she thought I would like and confided, "You know, Janet, I value artistic creativity more highly than anything else. I'd gladly have artistic talent in exchange for all those scholarly books with my name on them."

I was dumbfounded. "Would you, really? But I always think of you as the consummate academic, authoring all those books and exhibition catalogs during your years as department chair, university vice-provost, and now museum director."

"No. Like you, I was really interested in studio art as a teenager. But I wasn't talented enough. It was easy to be good at academics in comparison to the real creativity involved in being a good artist."

Ruth, for her part, kept insisting that my art making was a central part of the process of writing a book about Native American women and art.

"They are all related," she would say over and over to me, those words I needed to hear, in her indisputable college-professor voice. "Your knowledge of Native American weaving and beadwork and quillwork and basketry informs your quilt making. And your excursion into full-time quilt making will give you deeper insights into the artistry of those women, when you resume work on your book."

Yesterday, at home for just a few weeks since the trip, I lined up all my best Canyon de Chelly slides on the light table and sat down with paper and colored pencils. I do not intend to do a pictorial quilt, a direct translation of visual experience from one medium to another, but rather an abstract quilt. One that will evoke the colors and flavors of that day in the canyon. I thought about the three of us and drew three long rectangles on my pad. How about three interrelated wall hangings, each of which could stand alone, but together would evoke an even grander scene? Three totems (a particularly apt word, considering our profession), emblematic of a trio of women and their progress through a vivid autumnal landscape into the archaeological past.

It's a difficult problem in abstract design: to make three items that work together as a whole, each of which stands alone as a complete composition as well. I erase, sketch over, start again on a new sheet of paper.

I want to get up from my chair, make a cup of tea, walk the dogs, machine-stitch some other unfinished quilt.

Gestation is hard work.

I rest the abstract, problem-solving part of my brain by switching to the part that deals with colors. I pick through my two dozen bins of fabric and select some possible candidates for use in the quilt. These fabrics make other memories surface: the hand-dyed and hand-marbled fabrics in shades of copper, salmon, and sage green I bought from Sonya Lee Barrington, a vendor at last year's quilt show in Paducah, Kentucky; forest greens left over from the lap quilts I made Aldona and Ruth during the darkest, most miserable months of my depression last winter; some golds and yellows bought in the company of my other two sisters, the biological ones, Judith and B. J. Not all of the twenty-odd pieces I select will find their way into the textile, of course. But they represent the color palette and pattern range from which I will choose.

Creating a quilt has some predictable stages, like the stages of writing a book or falling in love. The first stage is splendid. My head is on fire with color and as-yet-unrealized patterns. I think about the quilt all the time, make notes and quick sketches, pull out fabric from the stash, and shop for new yardage too. I begrudge the time spent teaching, cooking, sleeping. I want to be alone with my embryonic ideas about the quilt.

The next stage is more structured. One plan must be selected out of all possibilities and refined. More sketches must be made, colors selected. But at this point, it must not be overdetermined. I can't know *exactly* what I'm going to do. There still must be ample room for surprise and serendipity.

Then the work gets easy for a while. For at least some period of time, cutting, stitching, and pressing will be relatively effortless. My body hums with excitement, but my mind is free to daydream about other things, listen to music, or just float in a nonverbal haze, entranced by pattern and color.

Then it gets hard again. Critical decisions must be made, a section redone or rejected. At this point I often neglect the work for a while. I fondle other fabrics, usually in a color range quite different from the one I'm working on. I read two novels back to back and write Christmas lists.

But then the quilt calls to me. I go upstairs to my study-studio one morning, planning to write a book review, and I sit down at the sewing machine instead. The quilt refuses to be neglected. I resume my relationship with it, and we work in harmony for a while.

Right now, in the Canyon de Chelly quilt, I am poised between initial elation and first inkling of dissatisfactions. But I am driven by this vision in my head that keeps me at the sketch pad, the pile of fabrics beside me. It is a vision of these three totemic forms on a wall somewhere. Perhaps they'll spend a year or two on a living-room wall in Fairbanks, Alaska, before being packed up and carried to a dining-room wall in Ottawa, Ontario, before their owner retrieves them to hang on a bedroom wall in St. Louis, Missouri.

DECEMBER 1993
Smashing the Dresden Plates

S everal years ago, while at an academic conference in South Dakota, I stole away from the tedium of slide lectures in darkened halls to cruise the antique shops downtown. In one, I found a stash of marvelous, pristine old quilt squares, reasonably priced.

I bought forty-two Butterflies and a tall stack of Dresden Plates in 1930s calicos.

I sewed the butterflies into a coverlet for the guestroom. Four years went by. Then I took out the Dresden Plates.

I've always liked the look of Dresden Plate Quilts. Their perky yet chalky colors are appealing: freewheeling, tiny patterns in pink, red, Wedgwood blue, green, and yellow. Dresden Plate Quilts are sunny quilts, made principally during the Depression, when times were tough. The Dresden Plates that I bought had been loosely basted to plain muslin, but not yet sewn down.

I wanted to make a quilt for my own bed, but I didn't like the chaste look of the calico circles on ivory muslin. I removed the basting threads and experimented with placing the plates onto modern fabrics in dark colors. I settled on a small basket-weave pattern in two shades of charcoal. I added some chalky pink speckled fabric as an accent color on borders and frames. Paradoxically, the vaguely Japanese look of my charcoal grays and muted pinks clashed with, as well as complemented, the '30s calicos. It was a slightly offbeat yet elegant choice (which is, come to think of it, a pretty good description of my aesthetic preferences—elegant yet unpredictable).

I topstitched a couple of the plates down on sixteen-inch gray squares. They floated there beautifully. (Unlike many Dresden Plate squares of the 1930s with their gaudy yellow centers, these plates had no centers. Their maker intended the plain off-white muslin below to serve as their centers. In truth, they look more like Dresden Jell-O molds than Dresden Plates.)

This project, like many of my Serendipity Quilts, had no preordained plan of action. I didn't know exactly where I was headed, and I liked it that way. But after floating three of these perfect rings with their riot of cheerful prints on that gray void, I knew that I didn't want my whole quilt to look like that.

I laid out a large piece of gray cloth on the floor and began to place the plates on it. The plates kept gravitating to the selvage of the cloth. They wanted to fly off the sides. I was stymied.

Then I heard a voice in my head. I didn't recognize it. It wasn't The

Nag, She-Who-Must-Be-Obeyed, who keeps up a running critical commentary. It said a surprising thing.

"Smash those plates."

That's heresy, I thought!

It said it again: "Smash the plates! They're your plates now."

Without too much thought, I picked up my rotary cutter and acrylic ruler and decisively cut through one of the plates.

Three slices. I didn't even flinch.

Now many of the charcoal gray squares have fragmentary plates on them. Sharp shards or petals, in clusters of seven, or four, or two. Some of these are stuffed with loose quilt batting to form a three-dimensional effect on the surface. Others are appliquéd flat. The large gray squares are separated by bands of Flying Geese in black and charcoal with pink or muted green backgrounds.

In terms of graphic design, it has movement, asymmetry, and visual interest that pulls your eye across the surface. It is also slightly mysterious, unsettling. Why all this fragmentary crockery, anyway?

In my daily life, I'm not much of a plate smasher. In fact, I can only remember two instances, about twenty years apart. During my senior year in college, I smashed a mug in fury against the kitchen cabinet after a particularly aggravating phone conversation with a man who was resisting my efforts to make him my boyfriend. And on Christmas Eve a year ago, I smashed my husband's glass flour canister while he was making Christmas breads for everyone else and refusing to pay attention to the sadness engulfing me.

In both instances, a single moment's action brought great psychic relief. The act of smashing banished the murk of despair.

My Smashed Plates Quilt is still unfinished. But I think I'm ready to take it out and complete it. With time's perspective, I see that I was doing more than smashing some South Dakota woman's plates. I was smashing my own intellectual china cabinet as well.

I felt an illicit thrill with that first slice. That thrill was a common feeling during the first few months of my quilting sabbatical, during which I was transgressing my own firm professorial code about maintaining at least banker's hours in my study, pursuing some scholarly project or another. Monday through Friday, 8 A.M. to 4 P.M., I'm "supposed to be" writing. This has been my pattern, assiduously practiced since 1978, when I began my doctoral dissertation and needed some framework so that I would know what hours I *had* to feel guilty and what hours I could allow myself to be free.

Those comfortable boundaries had become a prison and I needed to escape. Smash out. Not being able to write at all was certainly *one* defiant smashing of the established order. Quilting all day was another.

Smashing those plates marked a decisive moment. The realization came viscerally, not intellectually. It came by way of a daring act, a transgression with a rotary cutter.

It was the first definitive statement that I wasn't going to be operating within the old rules anymore. I was taking my rotary cutter and careening right off into the wilderness, where no signposts or speed limits marked the way.

Haven't come back yet.

DECEMBER 1993
The Sisters' Quilt

Perhaps it was the nineteenth-century Friendship Quilt which gave rise to the erroneous assumption that most historic American quilts were collective art works, made of scraps. Increasingly popular by the 1850s, groups of women would make identical piecework patches, often out of scrap fabrics, usually with a central piece of plain white muslin. Women inscribed their names, dates, and sentimental verses on the plain cloth in the center of the patchwork blocks. These keepsakes of female friendship were sometimes the only place where a woman's name was preserved in the nineteenth century, when governmental censuses often listed only the name of the "head of the household," usually male.

Friendship Quilts demonstrate the power of the bonds of female intimacy, often given as engagement presents or going-away presents. During the 1850s and 1860s, tens of thousands of women made the journey to a new life on the American frontier. When embarking upon the westward journey, people rightly assumed that they might never see their loved ones again. Friendship Quilts were an enduring sign of affection: literally blanketed by her friends, a nineteenth-century woman felt fortified for the perilous journey upon which she was embarking.

Within three months of taking up quilt making, I was eager to embark on a Friendship Quilt with my sisters, only we would call ours a Sisters' Quilt. When they came to St. Louis in November of 1992 to "usher me into my fifth decade" (as they insisted on calling my fortieth-birthday celebration), we went on an expedition to the fabric store and selected four fabrics that we all would use for the quilt blocks. We each chose a different fabric for our fifth fabric, to add variety and individuality to the blocks. (We paid for this fabric with the money our parents had sent to treat us all to dinner while we were together. This fulfilled the quilter's tradition of parsimony in some aspect of the project.)

We each made three blocks each of four different designs. We then shared the blocks, keeping one example of each of the four patterns we had done and receiving one of each of the four patterns the other sisters had made. From this exchange, each sister got twelve different blocks with which to make a quilt.

This was a humbling experience for me. My technical skills are not up to those of my sisters. My edges are not as straight, my star points don't meet as accurately and crisply at the seams. Yet I am brave and tend to plunge ahead, regardless. I made ambitious blocks: a Star inside a Pineapple, Jack in the Box, Dutchman's Puzzle, Red Skies at Night.

B. J. said, "You little whippersnapper! Always the precocious one!"

We agreed that our blocks would be completed by April 1993, when Judith and B. J. would again fly to St. Louis and we would drive to Paducah to attend the annual quilt celebration. Judith insisted that we exchange our blocks in Paducah, which made a memorable ritual out of it. We laid the blocks out on the carpet of our motel room and were speechless in front of the splendor of these little works. They were, in their own way, like us, as sisters. Made of the same fabric, but with subtle physical variations. All clearly related, yet each one unique.

I was the first to plunge into the task of setting my blocks into a pieced quilt top. As I played with my twelve blocks and arranged them in different ways on the floor, I took a lot of time making little sketches with colored pencils of possible arrangements. Should I enliven them by setting them in a complex interlocking border of flying geese? Should I break out of the grid entirely and set them in an unconventional pattern arrayed all over a fabric background?

At a Kansas City quilt show two months after the exchange of blocks, I attended a three-hour workshop titled "Creating Sparkling Sets." Its focus was on breaking through the normal expectation about sashing and borders—the cloth grid into which the pieced blocks are set—in order to create a more unusual framework or setting for the blocks. For example,

instead of

Even better, to try to blur the boundary between frame and block entirely by choosing elements of the block pattern that can be picked up and repeated in the setting.

From

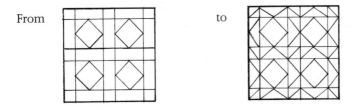

to

In either case the principles involve breaking through predictable, tired responses to a problem and finding new solutions.

What's left in my book manuscript is the setting of the "blocks" into an overall framework—putting together the many sections on different topics that I have written over the past few years and organizing them into an eloquent whole. And I have been scrupulously avoiding it. Instead, I have been obsessively quilting for months now.

I eventually settled on a very ambitious setting for some of my Sisters' blocks. Influenced by some of the illusionistic designs in Margaret Miller's book *Blockbuster Quilts*,[12] I wanted to make the blocks look like the front panels of a long, ribbonlike folding screen that would stand out on the picture plane. Illusionistic use of angle and color would make other parts of the screen recede. All of this would float on a background of shades of peach.

This would not only require new skills but also a great deal of patience, meticulous planning, and exacting execution. Not generally my strong points. I drew small-scale drawings on graph paper and enlarged them to a full-size, accurate pattern in four long strips, also on graph paper, whose precise measurements I would follow as I constructed the quilt top.

As I did all of this, part of me (the little part that usually perches on my shoulder and nags) stood back and was impressed: "Amazing!" she (I) said. "For months now you have been saying that what interested you the most about quilting is the freewheeling play of it, the improvisation. Yet here you are choosing a rigorous pattern, scaled down to the exact quarter inch to set your Sisters' blocks in. Not like you (me) at all." (Clearly, there is some confusion about whether I want to admit that this nag/critic/judge is part of me.)

This two-part process—first, trying to break through predictable ways of doing things and then rigorously organizing and painstakingly connecting—is the task I must now take up in my book manuscript. Quilters often have an unduly optimistic sense that "it's mostly done" once the blocks are pieced, but as every quilter can attest, one often expends as much time and energy on the last one-third of the project as on the first two-thirds. It's puzzling but true. No doubt there's some arcane law of physics that explains it.

The same principle holds true in the writing of books, as I know well from past experience. A book that is two-thirds written is really only half done. Editing, rewriting, filling in the gaps, and making a bridge of words between different sections of a manuscript is a very demanding process. Indeed, it's very much like accurately setting these various blocks into a quilt.

There is one large difference, however. In the quilt-making process I see it as fun. Granted, it is slow, deliberate fun. Because I have never attempted this sort of quilt setting before, it is a challenging sort of fun. I have fled from my book these past few months because in that arena I see it not as fun nor as a challenge, but as a torment. Why?

Planning the setting for the Sisters' blocks involves a lot of tedium and precision. Yet it also involves subtleties of color mixing as I join together four light apricot prints to make a soft background mosaic with an occasional bright star pieced into it. I need to convince myself that in a manuscript I can be equally proud of the way that I have solved the problem of eliding one section into another or the skillful manner in which I have set up a repeating pattern, a metaphor, or an image that carries through an entire chapter.

In quilting, this last stage requires the tools of colored pencils, paper patterns, graph paper, spray adhesive, tracing paper, and plenty of time to play. It requires seeing connections that are not obvious at first glance. It requires not only long hours of play, but of vision and re-vision. The result? A unique and meaningful whole, not boxed in but set free. Any kind of creative endeavor, from writing a book to planning a perennial garden to orchestrating a perfect meal, requires this same balance of skills.

Creating the Sisters' Quilt is a very different approach to quilt making than the Serendipity Quilts I described in "Piecing for Cover." Yet both are deeply satisfying. At some points in life's progress or a quilt's progress, the more freewheeling approach is needed. Other times and other endeavors require the more disciplined plan. It's important to keep all these skills in practice, all these mental muscles limber, in order to produce the most creative and diverse works that are within us.

I search through my slides and books to see how those nineteenth-century women did it: M. A. Knowles put together blocks made by other friends and church members and inscribed it to her "Sweet Sister Emma, 1843." She chose two types of intense, saturated yellow fabric to form the background blocks. The nine-patch Friendship blocks dance rhythmically across the yellow surface. Martha Ann placed her colored patches carefully, with an eye toward aesthetics: most of the red patches cluster in the center, while the more somber ones are placed around the edges.[13]

I only used seven of my twelve Sisters' blocks in my quilt. I don't know yet what I'll do with the others. This is the happy side of unfinished business. I'll hold on to them until some lonely day, then I'll let loose the creative warmth of my sisters to dance in patchwork around me.

JANUARY 1994

Delectable Mountains

S ome of the memorable names given to quilt patterns serve as little windows onto history. Fifty-Four Forty or Fight is an odd name for a pattern that combines four-patch and eight-pointed stars. It recalls America's determination during the War of 1812 to extend our northern border well into what is today Canada, beyond the fifty-fourth parallel. Radical Rose, the rose with a black center, was popular during the Civil War among those women who worked for the abolition of slavery.

Other names reflect the Christian devotion of many American quilt makers of the last two hundred years, such as Rose of Sharon, Walls of Jericho, Caesar's Crown, and Crown of Thorns. These all come directly from the Bible; other names are religious but don't stem from a biblical source. Robbing Peter to Pay Paul and Delectable Mountains are two that spring to mind.

I've always loved the name Delectable Mountains, just as I love the pattern by that name. The pattern is one of the thousand variations of small triangles of contrasting colors sewn together and sewn to the sides of a larger triangle. The name comes from the seventeenth-century inspirational book *Pilgrim's Progress*, in which it is written, "They went till they came to the Delectable Mountains which belong to the Lord."

For some quilters, this pattern evokes a holy pilgrimage and Christian devotion. My associations are different and wholly idiosyncratic. Saying "Delectable Mountains" makes my mouth water; delectable is a succulent word. A consultation with my Webster's Dictionary confirms this: "very pleasing, delightful, especially pleasing to the taste." Loving creative play in the kitchen almost as much as in the quilt studio, I decided to concoct a dessert called Delectable Mountains. Of what would it consist? I made notes of some possibilities, but none seemed exactly right. As I pondered, Bradley strolled in.

"If there were a dessert called Delectable Mountains, what would it be?" I demanded.

Never ruffled by the oddest of questions, my husband stopped and thought a moment. "It would look like Tom and Sophie's French wedding cake. What was that called?"

"*Croquembouche.*"

Bradley was thinking of the dessert extravaganza, traditional at French weddings, which was served at the wedding reception of our friends, one of whom is Parisienne. A tall mountain of individual little cream puffs glued together by caramelized sugar syrup, it is staggeringly sweet and rich. It is too far on the other side of delectable for my stomach.

"You are on the right track, but that's not it," I said.

"What about little mountains of meringues," Bradley offered. "My mother and I used to make meringues when I was small."

I nodded and began to write.

"We could hollow them out from the bottom, like we do with poached pears, and spoon some delectable surprise inside," he continued, always willing to take on a culinary challenge.

"Flecks of orange and lemon peel would make the meringues less bland," I added.

"Dark chocolate sauce," we both said.

I went into the kitchen and took down from the shelf my dog-eared and brown-edged copy of *Fanny Farmer*, bought in 1973, and my only slightly less careworn *Joy of Cooking*. (It seemed only right to stick with these plain, American classics for such an undertaking.) I consulted their instructions for meringues. *Joy of Cooking* mentioned that meringues are seldom successful in humid weather. It was a steamy

August afternoon in St. Louis. Today, the first day of 1994, we made our Delectable Mountains.

Delectable Mountains
MERINGUES

4 egg whites, at room temperature
¼ teaspoon cream of tartar
1 cup sifted confectioner's sugar
1 tablespoon finely diced lemon and orange peel

Preheat oven to 225°F.
Butter and flour a cookie sheet.

In a glass or stainless steel bowl (not plastic) whip the egg whites and cream of tartar using an electric mixer at high speed. As egg whites begin to thicken, start adding the sugar, a little bit at a time. Continue to whip, patiently, until mixture forms stiff peaks. (This might take 10–15 minutes.) During the last 2–3 minutes of whipping, add finely diced lemon and orange peel.

Spoon mixture onto prepared baking sheet, dividing it into six "mountains."

Bake in low oven for at least 1 hour. Meringues will turn light beige on the outside, but should not wiggle. Turn heat off. Let meringues cool in the oven for 10 minutes. Take out and remove from cookie sheet with a thin metal spatula.

If you want some chocolate sauce inside the mountain, now is the time to use your finger to break a hole in the underside of the meringue mountains before they cool completely.

Cool on wire rack or big serving platter.

CANDIED LEMON AND ORANGE PEEL (FOR GARNISH)

One lemon
One orange, both well scrubbed
½ cup sugar
waxed paper

Using a carrot peeler, peel long strips (2–3 inches long) from the skins of one lemon and one orange. Try not to take too much of the white pith underneath the skin.

Using a thin, sharp knife, cut these strips into long slivers less than ⅛ inch wide. You should have approximately ½ cup loosely packed citrus slivers. (Whatever small, odd-shaped pieces you have left over can be diced fine for the peel needed in the meringue mixture.)

Boil 1 cup water in a small saucepan. Put the long slivers of citrus peel in the water and let boil for 3–4 minutes. Drain, add another cup of water, and repeat. Drain ⅔ of the water.

To the citrus slivers and remaining ⅓ cup water, add ½ cup sugar. Continue to boil until water evaporates and sugar syrup glazes all the peels. Using a fork, lift and separate the peels and then place them to dry on a piece of waxed paper. (Careful! Sugar syrup is hot and sticks to skin!)

CHOCOLATE SAUCE

2 squares unsweetened baker's chocolate (2 ounces)
1 tablespoon dry cocoa powder
1 tablespoon butter
3 tablespoons cream
½ cup sugar (approx.)

In top of double boiler set over (not into) simmering water, melt the butter into the cream. Whisk in the cocoa powder. Break up the chocolate squares with a knife and add to the mixture, whisking occasionally.

After all is melted and mixed, begin to whisk in the sugar to taste. Keep in mind that the meringues themselves are very sweet, so a bitter chocolate rather than a sweet chocolate flavor is desirable here. Simmer for several minutes.

If made in advance, store in a glass jar, and heat lightly by microwaving for 20 seconds or so.

Place a meringue on each of six plain dessert plates.

(Note: If you want a chocolate surprise inside the meringue mountains, hold a meringue mountain upside down in your hand. Pour a spoonful of chocolate into the cavity you formed when the meringues were cooling. Invert dessert plate over the mountain, and using both hands, turn plate and meringue mountain right side up.)

Drizzle the warmed chocolate sauce over each meringue, in a manner that looks pleasing to you.

Sprinkle the candied lemon and orange peel slivers over the tops of the mountains.

Serve at once, atop your best quilted place mats.

The pathways to creativity are unpredictable. I've gone from the literary exploration of a name, to the culinary experiment that I hope lives up to the vivid image evoked by the phrase "Delectable Mountains." Now, to take the inquiry full circle, perhaps I shall pay homage to that recipe by making a quilted wall hanging.

It will have creamy whites that recall the mountains of meringues. Small triangles of yellow and orange are the tangy citrus accents. Rich dark browns evoke the chocolate sauce. In the spirit of parsimony, I will use my leftover browns from Kevin Eckstrom's quilt, and I will borrow from my stash of yellows that are my hedge against the loss of my husband. In the spirit of extravagance, I will run right out tomorrow and buy a selection of creams and oranges that will be more than ample for this experiment and will enrich my fabric stash for years to come.

Pansies for My Mother, 1

A few months ago, I bought a quarter yard each of two different Hoffman fabrics printed with pansies. One sports blue and white pansies, with a navy background, the other, purple and yellow pansies on black. On both, the pansies are edged with shiny gold. My mother loves pansies. I have never made her a quilted gift. I thought I might try.

After almost thirty years of keeping my distance from her, I wanted to try to honor those memories I have of our happy times, memories of being four years old, at home with her during the day. She would make me orange sherbet to eat before my nap. Broken pieces of Hershey chocolate bar, a special surprise, would be hidden inside the cold sherbet. I have strong memories of planting pansies together in the side yard of the house we lived in then, on Summer Street in Fitchburg, Massachusetts. My mother still loves pansies; they adorn her jewelry and stationery. I love them too, plant them in my yard, and serve them in composed salads. Love of this simple flower is one of our few commonalities.

I was born when my mother was forty, a decade after the birth of Judith. I'm sure I was a surprise, and probably not an entirely welcome one. B. J. remembers hearing crying and yelling behind closed doors the summer before I was born.

My mother is eighty-one now, though to me she looks much the same as she has for twenty years. She still dyes her hair brown and wears long, flowered scarves and costume jewelry to dress up her practical pants suits in navy or brown. When I was a child in the 1950s and early 1960s, I found her rather glamorous. She wore long black gloves, large, veiled hats, spike-heeled shoes, and sheath dresses. Her clothing smelled of Chanel Number Five or White Shoulders. She worked full time in an office. I didn't know any other mothers who worked full time.

My mother grew up in a small town in central Massachusetts, a factory town. She was the third eldest daughter in a large French-Canadian family. Her father was a Realtor and had attended college, so the family thought themselves superior to their neighbors. The children were held to strict moral codes. Appearances were everything, as they still are to my mother.

Academically precocious, she completed high school at a Catholic boarding school in two years. After she graduated at fifteen, there was no thought of sending this, the brightest child, off to college; in 1928 a dutiful French-Canadian girl went to work in an office and contributed money to the family so that her younger brothers could attend college. One of her older sisters escaped this stifling atmosphere by entering the convent and getting an education there; another eloped, pregnant. My mother, Jeannette (or Jane, as she always called herself—a spare, modern name), didn't marry until she was twenty-three. But she was a small-town sophisticate who took trips to New York with her sister, smoked an occasional cigarette, and loved the glamorous, urbane world of the movies. I have a photo of her at age twenty, in 1932. She is lounging on the fender of my father's Ford V-8 touring car. In her fur-collared coat and kid gloves, she looks like a movie star herself.

My intellectual abilities are a legacy from both my parents. My father is good with figures and mechanical things; my mother worked for many years as an executive secretary and proofreader. Her vocabulary and eye for language are superb. While not, strictly speaking, artistic, she has always had a great sense of style. She loves fine, well-tailored clothes, made of good-quality fabrics. Each of her daughters inherited her flair for dressing. Each of us has her weakness for too many clothes and too expensive shoes.

As a woman who worked full time, Jane had her own money and spent it as she saw fit. Often it was on special outfits for her girls, or Sunday dinner in a restaurant for the whole family, or a little money tucked into the pocket of her brother, the priest. From her, I learned a certain generosity of spirit. My mother was the one who treated my cousins and me to hot fudge sundaes at Bailey's after a day of shopping in Boston or bought my best friend a matching blouse when she bought mine.

Jane never had enough money to buy expensive furniture or to have an ostentatious home, but she loved fine china, thick towels, fresh bars of soap, and gaily patterned sheets. My childhood was full of these small extravagances. My dress-up outfits were purchased at Best's or Franklin Simon or Bonwit Teller, shops that were really too costly for our working-class family but where end-of-season sales provided excellent bargains.

My mother lost her way for a few years in her fifties. She cut herself off from her large, extended family and threw herself into her work. My sisters had already left home, but my own adolescence coincided with her explosive menopause. It was a dramatic, emotional, depressive affair for us both. She fought with me unceasingly, and she turned against my sweet father, whose simplicity and reticence infuriated her. Her sisters had smooth, gregarious husbands who drove Cadillacs, had managerial jobs, and spacious houses. (One of these men was a mean-tempered drunk; another beat his wife. But the outward appearances were of a seamless middle-class existence. And appearances, remember, are everything.)

My relationship with my mother never recovered from those tempestuous years. Emotionally, I have put away this part of my youth, like a trunk full of fading quilt squares imprisoned in a stifling attic. But as she ages, I want to honor her. Because of my own emotional distance from her, it has to be in some expressive but un-self-revealing way. Cloth is an excellent medium for this. So I shall make her a wall hanging of precise pineapple blocks in which pansies take the place of that delicate flower that is my heart.

JANUARY 1994

(Black) Pansies for My Mother, 2

P art of the process of therapy for me these last few months has been to share some of these essays with my psychiatrist. At first it was simply sharing the fact of having written at all, after many arid months. But it quickly became apparent that my writing and the analytic sessions were intertwined.

In several instances, Dr. Snider thought I should deepen my word portraits, rather than simply being satisfied with a brief sketch. For

Christmas, I gave her a gift basket with fine delicacies nestled in raffia inside an ash-splint basket bedecked with straw sunflowers. Shortly after Christmas, she commented that I had a talent for packaging and presenting things beautifully, and that this talent was evident not only in the gift I had given her but also in my essays.

"However," she continued, "sometimes the presentation is too neat, too careful. You are leaving out the messiness. Some of these essays might be enriched by allowing the messiness in."

That afternoon I came home and wrote this essay in a white heat. It unfolded by itself on my computer screen, without going through the usual hesitant and much-erased first draft on paper. I started with the first two paragraphs of the previous essay and let the messiness emerge. It was a frightening experience.

I offer both versions here. As anyone who has had a deeply conflicted relationship with a parent knows, these essays don't contradict each other; each tells some truths. They must stand in counterpoise, like the intricate alternation of a quilt pattern, to tell my whole truth.

A few months ago, I bought a quarter yard each of two different Hoffman fabrics printed with pansies. One has blue and white pansies, with a navy background, the other, purple and yellow pansies on black. On both, the pansies are edged with shiny gold. My mother loves pansies. I have never made her a quilted gift. I thought I might try.

(The first clue to the stinginess of our relationship with each other shows even here. I never buy just a quarter yard of fabric. I am profligate in a quilt shop: a yard or two of anything that remotely interests me; a guarded quarter yard for her.)

After almost thirty years of a cold heart toward her, I had thought I might try to honor those few memories I have of happy times with her, memories of being four or five, at home with her during the day. She would make me orange sherbet to eat before my nap. Broken pieces of Hershey chocolate bar, a special surprise, would be hidden inside the cold sherbet. I have memories of planting pansies together in the side yard of the house we lived in then, on Summer Street in

Fitchburg, Massachusetts. My mother still loves pansies; they adorn her jewelry and stationery. I love them too, plant them in my yard, and serve them in composed salads. Love of this simple flower is one of the few commonalities I will allow us.

I left home at seventeen, after four emotionally brutal years of battle with my mother. When I went off to college, I took everything that was meaningful with me. I knew I was never coming back for more than a weekend. Perhaps one of the reasons I became an academic was that I found such solace, clarity, and salvation in my life in the university. A life of ideas, of art, of exploration of subtleties and feelings: This stood in contrast to my teenage years of battles, silences, criticisms, and craziness.

Directions for the pansy quilt to hang in my house
The background is a field of pansies, cut and shredded on the diagonal, sewn down roughly, with frayed edges showing. Portions of the field are covered with black nylon net, sewn over haphazardly. Inside the net are trapped pieces of cut up ribbons.

On the field is appliquéd one of my favorite patterns, Heart in Hand. The large hand is black. It is my hand. The front side of the stuffed heart attached to it is black. The heart fastens to the hand with a hook and eye.

(fragment of a Margaret Atwood poem from the 1970s)
We fit together like a hook and eye.
A fish hook. An open eye.

If you unhook the heart, you see that the back of it is patterned in purple and yellow pansies. Around where it is hooked to the hand, the hand fabric has been burned. Small burns, done with matches, leaving seared brown stuffing and fabric edges.

Directions for the pansy quilt to give to her
It will be a pineapple pattern, with regular, precise, geometric rows of pansies rhythmically encircling a central field of green.

Sewn inside the quilt, where she can't see it, are pieces of my diaries and letters: they are like the paper pieces sewn into late nineteenth-century crazy quilts to reinforce the fabric. A black raw-silk lining hides them from her. They are from different stages of my life.

Diary pages I wrote when I was fourteen, in a notebook I kept at school because I was "not allowed" to have a diary.

"Don't ever write anything down that you wouldn't want the whole world to see," she advised me angrily when I was eleven, after confiscating my diary.

Letters and poems I wrote at seventeen when, in the miasma of her own craziness, my mother burned my art work and my sheer, embroidered peasant blouses that my best friend had brought me from Mexico. I was founder and editor of *Mirage*, the literary magazine at my high school. Though I never showed the first issue of it to her, she found it in my room and read my poem about my boyfriend breaking off our relationship.

Her angry comment: "What do you think his parents thought when they read that?"

Diary entries at twenty-one, when I had an abortion and set off for Greece and then graduate school, alone. They chronicle the dreams I had of a little girl who needed saving. I was supposed to save her but I couldn't. I was that girl, little and big both.

Diary entries at thirty-two, when I left my first husband; at thirty-five, when my lover left me; blank pages at forty, locked in depression. Fragments of all these will be the reinforcing papers that allow me to sew precisely the careful design I have chosen. The papers will be torn into pieces, so that if she should slit the quilt open, she won't have too much information to use against me. Just the mysterious, unrevealing shards of my life.

Parsimony and Extravagance

N ative American women's arts often evince the same balance of parsimony and extravagance found in many American quilts. Traditional Eskimo women, for example, will talk about how vital it is to use every bit of nature's bounty. Rita Pitka Blumenstein, an Eskimo artist from southeastern Alaska, relates:

> In respect for the fish and the seal, you use every bit of it: the head, the insides, the bones, and the skin of the fish. And then whatever we don't eat goes to the dogs. The bones go back to the river or the lake, wherever you caught it from. If they're from the ocean, you take them there. That will ensure more fish in the next years. If it's a seal, same way. The bladder goes back to the sea. The seals will come back. You bury the bones near the sea, so you won't find them floating all over the beach. I appreciate very much the respect for things when I was growing up. So you use every bit of it—the bones for tools, the insides for clothing, eat the kidney and liver and the meat. Use the seal oil also. The stomach is used for storing the seal oil and for when you gather salmonberries. The skin you use for parkas, mittens, or mukluks. The bones you use for scrapers, runners for sleds and for tanning. The whiskers are used for toothpicks and the faces are used for ornaments. The bladder goes back to the sea.[14]

Northern women even grew proficient in using fish skin for patchworklike ornamentation of clothing and bags!

During the reservation period at the end of the nineteenth century, many Plains Indian women began to do an obsessive, extravagant style of all-over beadwork, covering entire dresses, valises, vests, and other items with a dense tapestry of beads. Sometimes moccasins were completely beaded on the soles as well as on the uppers. In this artistic explosion we can read many facts about reservation-era culture: the prohibition of traditional lifeways and ceremonies meant that women had more time for artistry. Moreover, women's arts were more important than ever as carriers of cultural meaning, as other avenues of cultural expression were closed.

I find this balancing act between parsimony and extravagance particularly successful in quilts. Some see only their parsimonious aspects. One year, when I taught a college seminar on women's arts and spent the whole first month of the class on quilts and their central position in women's culture, one brash nineteen-year-old feminist let loose with her impatience:

"Scraps! That's all women are ever allotted in our patriarchal culture! Scraps! I'm sick of it and I don't think we should celebrate it."

It was one of the few times I've been stunned into silence in the classroom. Although in some senses she wasn't wrong, her analysis was so utterly reductive, so simplistic, that I didn't know how to begin to address it. As I think of it now, perhaps shaming her with her own jargon would have made her think. I should have pointed out that to look at quilts and see only scraps is to wear the most constricting of patriarchal blinders.

Undeniably, there is the aspect to quilting that is the material equivalent to the Pollyannaish phrase, "if life gives you lemons, make lemonade." Make do with what you've got, no matter how meager. But looked at from another perspective, parsimony of materials poses some excellent design challenges. Economic circumstances forced many a nineteenth-century quilt maker to make do with what she had. This caused her to come up with marvelous, resourceful designs.

The earliest American quilts seem to have been made of large pieces of whole cloth stitched together into a "sandwich." The surface of this blanket would then be covered by a subtle layer of imagery laboriously formed by hand, using needle and thread to work patterns of vines, flowers, or geometric designs. In the late eighteenth and early nineteenth centuries, imported cloth was expensive, and except among the wealthiest, was usually combined with local hand-spun cloth in quilts. The parsimonious use of treasured bits of chintz (a costly import from Great Britain or India) contrasted with the extravagance of the thousands of quilting stitches that would decorate the surface of such a textile.

In 1826, fourteen-year-old Sarah Johnson of eastern Pennsylvania made her fourth quilt.[15] Its central medallion was composed of hundreds of bits of fabric in a complex design. Radiating out from this is a repeating geometric pattern of blocks of colored eight-pointed stars alternating with plain white squares. This use of white blocks as a background against which the pieced squares stand out was a design innovation of nineteenth-century American quilters, who found in it an endlessly fascinating and changeable repertory of geometric play. Sarah Johnson surrounded her quilt with a border of pieced triangles known as "flying geese." This, in turn, is bordered by bands of orange and pink that enclose the whole design field.

Johnson composed her quilt from more than four thousand individual pieces of fabric. Those fabrics in the pieced stars are probably scraps leftover from the family's dressmaking, though certainly the white fabric in the plain squares, the pink and orange borders, and the backing would have been purchased by the yard, expressly for this project.

It would not have been uncommon in the nineteenth century for a fourteen-year-old to have completed four ambitious quilts, as Sarah Johnson did. Little girls mastered simple hand-sewing techniques by the age of four or five and were proficient needlewomen just a few years later, as numerous surviving embroidered samplers demonstrate. In the colonial economy, such skills were a practical necessity, for all members contributed economically to the household through hard work, even the youngest ones. By the 1820s, however, with the rise of a larger middle class, women's skills were directed more to "fancy work" than to plain work. So Sarah's extravagant use of white blocks and the proud display of her deft hand with a quilting needle, contradict the parsimony in the scrap stars.

In my own piecework, I embrace parsimony as a design challenge. It is a way of paying homage to the enforced frugality of the nineteenth-century quilter. Sometimes I make quilts out of the discards from other projects.

I like to make flying geese using Diana McClun's and Laura Nownes's method, as described in *Quilts! Quilts! Quilts!*,[16] sewing small squares diagonally on either side of a larger rectangle, trimming off the triangular corners. This results in beautifully straight and regular Flying Geese. According to some quilters, it is an extravagant method, because you use more fabric than you would if you pieced the geese another, more time-consuming way, using just smaller and larger triangles. Yet there is a double benefit to my preferred method. Not only are the geese perfect and crisp looking, but you are left with corner triangles that you cut off and—discard? No! They are already matched up with a contrasting fabric, right sides together. You stitch them together as they are, resulting in little diagonally pieced squares ready for another project, such as Bear's Paw, Delectable Mountain, or Feathered Star. I made my first Bear's Paw this way.

B. J. often makes Flying Geese borders but is too impatient to stitch and iron all those tiny triangle discards. Now she saves them all for me. B. J. often comes to visit, bearing two or three plastic Ziploc sandwich bags full of triangles, in patterns or colors that I would not have chosen but with which I am eager to play. This results in a sort of "parsimony squared," for not only are these tidbits the detritus of another project, they are someone else's discards, and so they are free.

But if parsimony is one of the aesthetic strategies of piecework, extravagance is another. They are inextricably intertwined.

Every one of us has heard of the churlish husband (always someone else's, of course!) who complains, "But, honey, I don't understand it. Why would you take all this perfectly good fabric, cut it to pieces, and sew it back together. It's such a waste!"

And he has a point. It is extravagant, of both time and materials to engage in this odd pursuit. But we've been doing it for a couple hundred years now, and piecework shows no indication of dying out any time soon. But the mere cutting and piecing is the least of the many extravagances found in quilt making.

The tens of thousands of fine hand-quilting stitches that cover many quilts are an extravagant display of talent. Moreover, they indicate that the needlewoman has patience to spare as well.

If the blocks are hand pieced, the amount of time spent in putting them together seems particularly extravagant in the modern world, when we can feed multiple pieces through the sewing machine so rapidly.

Sometimes the sheer number of conjoined pieces is an indication of the extravagance of the quilter's vision and industry. In the twenty-five years after 1850, Nancy Osborn and Eva Besemer pieced 21,559 triangles to form their Broken Dishes Quilt.[17] In a Flower Basket petit-point-style quilt made by Grace Snyder in Nebraska in the 1940s, a staggering 85,875 little squares were joined with over 5,400 yards of thread.[18]

To many modern quilters, myself included, the biggest extravagance is one we take for granted: being able to go to the fabric store where we may find as many as five hundred bolts of excellent quality cotton material. To buy a half yard of one, a quarter yard of yet another, three full yards of a pattern that is particularly pleasing is a great delight.

In the mid-nineteenth century, the invention of aniline dyes, a new screen-printing process for fabric, and mercerized thread made high-quality materials relatively inexpensive and easily available. This ushered in a great explosion in the art of quilting. While popular accounts always talk about scraps and making do, it is clear that many nineteenth-century quilts, especially those made by urban, middle-class women, were planned in advance, with enough fabric bought to complete a preconceived design (like Sarah Johnson's, previously mentioned).

To a less affluent countrywoman, purchasing yard goods in large amounts was thrilling, a rare extravagance. In *The Quilters*, one elderly Texas woman recalls her mother taking her into town to get a few small pieces of calico to renew the scrap bag:

We had picked three pieces of remnant blue and was just fingerin' some red calico. We was jest plannin' on enough for the middle squares from that.

Just then Papa come in behind us and I guess he saw us lookin.' He just walked right past us like he wasn't with us, right up to the clerk and said, "How much cloth is on that bolt?"

The clerk said, "Twenty yards."

Papa never looked around, He just said, "I'll take it all!"

He picked up that whole bolt of red calico and carried it to the wagon. Mama and me just laughed to beat the band. Twenty yards of red. Can you imagine?[19]

For rural, poor African-American women who didn't have much, it was the thrill of bold color and wild pattern that led to the extravagant design aesthetic of southern Black quilt making. These quilts were long unappreciated, because they seemed to lack the rigor and control valued so highly in the Anglo-American quilt tradition for most of its history. Yet their design aesthetic is a legacy from ancestral West Africa. What art historian Robert Farris Thompson has called "high-affect color collisions" form the basis for their visual extravagance and assertion. Lucinda Toomer's Bear's Paw Quilt, made in Georgia in 1979, when the quilter was eighty-nine years old, displays nine Bear's Paw patterns in bold red, blue, check, and plaid. They are set within a colorful asymmetrical grid. Some of the paws are mismatched, some of their sawtooth edges are reversed. It is an exuberant firecracker of a quilt.[20]

Silk, satin, ribbon, velveteen, all overlaid in lush profusion—the extravagance of the Crazy Quilt took America by storm in the 1880s. This led to a sermonizing editorial in Harper's Bazar magazine in 1884, which suggested that the mania for making Crazy Quilts "stood for a misdirected energy and perseverance too common among women."[21] (The author suggested instead that such prodigious amounts of time might better be directed at learning painting, a foreign language, poetry, or "the important science of housekeeping and kitchen chemistry.")

Our culture is full of lots of tiresome stereotypes about women, a fair number of them revolving around issues of parsimony and extravagance. Women are alleged to be cheap at tipping waiters. (In my experience, women are more likely to have *been* waiters, and so we tend to leave 20 percent no matter what!)

Some men believe the stereotype of women as extravagant creatures, spending wildly on cosmetics and clothes. Maybe some women live up to these stereotypes, but most quilters don't. If I see a designer jacket I "need" to have, and it is a good quality one, marked down to $150, I might try it on. But when I weigh it on my mental scale against the visual image of $150 worth of fabric (truly a formidable stack!) the suit jacket usually goes right back on the rack.

Today a wealth of materials on the shelves at home is the one extravagance in which many quilters indulge. To have a generous stash is to be wealthy in the riches that quilters prize.

Often, as I write and piece, I realize that I am working out patterns in my life as well. As I write this, it becomes staggeringly obvious to me that my own emotional life as a child careened back and forth between the poles of parsimony and extravagance. With money, my father was parsimonious, and my mother extravagant. And they certainly perpetuated this pattern in response to the extremity of each other's actions. My mother's wild swings of emotion were exaggerated, especially in the face of my father's reserve and restraint. In contrast, my father was the spendthrift when it came to patience and love for his daughters. There, unfortunately, my mother was the tightwad.

Perhaps it is a sign of maturity that I am finally beginning to recognize that my own relationship with my parents has long hinged on these two extremes: I've been emotionally parsimonious toward my mother since my early adolescence, while at the same time, acting extravagantly, uncritically loving toward my father.

In life and in art, I walk the line between parsimony and extravagance, not always getting the balance right.

FEBRUARY 1994
The Strip Quilt

M y father almost died last month. Nearly eighty-four, he is suffering from advanced emphysema. When my sister Judith went to my parents' apartment to visit early in January, she found him more feeble than ever before. Concerned about my mother's ability to cope, Judith stayed. She sat up with my father all night, as he struggled to breathe, unable to do so despite his oxygen line. He gasped and choked for breath.

In the morning an ambulance took him to the hospital, his condition so poor that the ambulance attendants wanted to put him on a respirator. "No," he said. He had all the legal papers to back up his terse refusal, and Judith was there to see that his wishes were obeyed.

Judith called that evening. "Time to come."

I flew to New England in the middle of a wretched winter snowstorm stretching from St. Louis to Maine. I made it successfully to Philadelphia, changing planes and taking off just before that airport closed. I landed in Manchester, New Hampshire, during the brief period when the airport had reopened; shortly thereafter it closed again.

B. J. met me at the airport, which is very close to her home. We intended to drive down to Boston, but by then the interstate highway was impassable. We went to B. J.'s house and waited for the storm to lift.

I wondered if I would see my father alive again.

Another fifteen inches of snow fell, from that night into the next day. I felt jittery, impotent, trapped. B. J. was living with other people now; I was conscious of being a guest in the home of strangers rather than family in my sister's home. I retreated to the quiet of her quilting studio, hoping to calm myself with a project, any project.

In an effort to create order and space in her new studio, B. J. was throwing away some old fabrics, leftover strips and squares from various endeavors. While my generous sister would have let me take anything I wanted from her bountiful shelves of yardage, I chose fragments from the discard bags. There were lots of strips in beige, rose, brown, and rust, from her many Log Cabin and Trip Around the World commissions. The strips ranged from 1 ¼ inches to 3 inches in width. I set myself the task of making a Strip Quilt. African-American quilters, especially southern ones, sometimes call these "String Quilts." They represent the ultimate in frugality. Often made up of worn-out pajama tops, aprons, skirt fabric, and pieces too narrow to cut a triangle or block from, they are the last stop for all sorts of odds and ends.

In another discard bag I found a pile of five-inch tobacco-colored calico squares. I decided to use them to punctuate the strip pattern at asymmetrical intervals. The only thing I chose from the new fabric stash was a half yard of black print Hoffman cotton to provide some emphatic visual syncopation amid the lighter colored strips. With almost no cutting to do, I began to piece right away, putting together strips of various widths, capping the sections off with a five-inch mustard square.

As I did this, of course, I thought about my father and the impenetrable barrier of snow, sixty miles wide, that separated us. A man of few words, and not demonstrative, he loves his three girls fiercely. It is a simple, uncomplicated love. Unlike our mother's, it is not tainted by judgment or criticism. He is always pleased to see us and enjoys the sunny, teasing love we give to him. For our love for him, too, is simple and uncritical. We are happy in each other's presence—it is as simple as that.

This Strip Quilt is emblematic of my father in several ways. Much of his clothing is rust, brown, and beige. He is generous with his daughters but frugal in his personal habits. Like many people who weathered the Great Depression, he saves rubber bands on doorknobs and accumulates scrap paper and other odds and ends that might be useful "someday." He would approve of the idea of using up scraps and making them into something practical rather than discarding them.

As the snow came down that day and into the next, I worked obsessively on my strip quilting, trying to use it as a meditative practice, to calm me in a more constructive way than the stash of Xanax I had on hand for this crisis. I thought of my daddy as I pieced and ironed, pieced and ironed.

For a brief period in my childhood, I craved a *Father Knows Best* kind of daddy, wise and all-knowing, who would call me "kitten." My father never called me anything but Janet. (Well—that's not true. A dozen times in the last twenty years, since I embarked on the road to fellowships, advanced degrees, and professorships, a road he values but does not understand very well, he has called me his "pride and joy.")

My father worked two jobs during most of my childhood. He was a high-precision machinist for W. R. Grace Company all day, and he had a series of odd jobs after work. Most revolved around cars. He helped his friend who owned a gas station. He performed auto repairs for a wide circle of acquaintances. Later he kept the books for another friend's auto supply shop. He always put money away, ten and twenty dollars at a time, ensuring a more comfortable retirement for my mother and him. Ensuring that even in his eighties he could buy a new car and pay cash for it. Ensuring that he would always be able to take a crisp stack of twenties out of his wallet and pay for Sunday dinner for the whole family. That's what gave him pleasure.

This quilt is a modest looking thing, almost homely. Neither loud nor elegant nor refined, it is very comforting. My father's love is like that. It expresses itself in practicality rather than in extravagance: buying new tires for B. J.'s car; methodically removing the discoloration from Judith's copper-bottomed pans with steel wool and some mysterious automotive scouring solution; slipping a twenty-dollar bill and a note in an envelope to me when I was away at college, working my way through and always short of funds.

The most extravagant thing my father ever did for me was still a highly practical gesture. Having borrowed a truck to transport my belongings to New Haven as I was about to begin graduate school, he helped me move into my new apartment. We settled everything in, and then he said, almost gruffly, "Come on now, we are going to go to the supermarket and get you everything you need to set this place up."

We walked together down the supermarket aisles, him pushing the cart. It was not an unusual feeling, for we had grocery shopped together often throughout my childhood. He scanned every shelf for something I might need. I was inclined to limit myself to the basics and leave it at that. He wanted me to have the works: flour, sugar, cornmeal, canned soups, spices. We stopped in front of the little jars of herbs and spices.

"Now, come on, get everything that you use in cooking. How about basil? Don't you need basil? Cardamom seed? Do you use fennel seed?" He read the unfamiliar names from the jars.

"Don't you need more cleaning supplies than this? Better get some extras so you won't have to lug them yourself on the bus."

We walked out of that supermarket laden with at least a half-dozen big brown-paper bags of groceries. My father was satisfied that I would not starve, on my own in this new city. Only then was he content to drive his borrowed truck back to Boston.

He seemed so old to me that September of 1974, when he was sixty-four and I was twenty-one. Now, from the vantage point of his hospital bed, where he is thin and spent, with blue, cracked lips and an oxygen tube in his nose, an I.V. line in his arm, I look back and see instead his vigor.

All of my subunits of cloth strips form bands about 5 inches wide. I connect them, and before long I have three-quarters of a quilt top made, in just a day and a half. In between bouts of shoveling twenty-six inches of snow off the cars and out of the long driveway, I continue obsessively to stitch and remember.

My father's name is Bernard. Bernie. We are all J. B.'s and B. J. B.'s in our family: Bernard, Jeannette, B. J., Judith, Janet.

When he was seventy-nine, my father tried to work on my car. It was the first and last time. I had bought my BMW 320i new in St. Louis ten years before. I had sent photos, and he had seen it on subsequent car trips I made to the East Coast. But this year I was on sabbatical, living in Rhode Island. It was the first time that I lived close enough for him to get his hands under the hood. He had worked on American cars since 1923, owned his own new Model A Ford when he was nineteen, in 1929, but he appreciated fine foreign engineering too. He even bought a book on BMWs and studied up, before he attempted to teach me how to give my car a tune up. (How I wished I had paid attention during my high school years, when he would so willingly have taught me the arcane ways of car maintenance!)

His hands were dry and cracked, and crippled up with arthritis in a way I had not noticed before. My father's big, capable hands. He no longer had the strength to loosen easily the valves and nuts with his tools, a new, metric set, bought expressly for my German car. He gave them to me to keep in the trunk.

We gave that car a tune-up, by God. It took us all afternoon in the parking lot of the little apartment building where he and my mother lived. There were times I thought we'd have to give up and call a mechanic to tow us in. He huffed and puffed, his emphysema getting the best of him even then, ten years after he'd stopped smoking.

We adjusted the timing. We changed the spark plugs. We did a host of other things that I don't remember now. He had bought all the supplies wholesale, at the automotive store where still, at seventy-nine, he worked part-time as the sole inventory clerk. (When he retired a year later, they had to invest in an expensive, computerized inventory system to do the job he had done for ten years with simple filing cards and his precise notations.)

When we finished, the car wouldn't start. He looked as dejected as I had ever seen him. I understood for the first time the impotence of old age, when your hands and your lungs and your muscle strength betray you, even though just under the surface lurks the boy of nineteen whose mechanical talents are prodigious and who likes nothing better than to spend an afternoon in the sunshine, fiddling under the hood of a car.

I doubt that any car had ever defeated him before. And I was sorry that the occasion of his defeat had to be my car. He, of course, was mortified and apologetic to me. I had brought him a running vehicle, and now we couldn't even get the engine to turn over.

"Well, I dunno," he said listlessly. "Let's try something else."

We sat there for a minute longer, he behind the wheel, I in the passenger seat beside him. He caught his breath and flexed his swollen knuckles. He wiped his hands on a rag, pulled himself up, and ducked under the hood again. More mysterious fiddling. The spark plugs, I think.

"Okay, Janet, you try it now. But go easy on the gas."

The engine roared to life, idling better than it had in years. The grim look left his face, replaced by a wide grin. He hadn't been bested by a car, after all. We stowed the extra spark plugs, oil filter, timing meter, rags, and metric socket wrenches in the trunk. We took the car for a spin. I don't recall what I thought at the time, but in retrospect, in my sentimental mood now, it reminds me of our drives together when I was a little girl. On visits to Aunt Caroline, or out on errands, I always got a treat: an ice cream cone, a ginger ale, perhaps a bag of

M&Ms. He was in his late forties and early fifties then, his hidden wildness doing battle with his caution. He would rev the engine at red lights, jump the gun at green ones, and race through yellow ones. On the parkway we would drive far faster than the speed limit.

I was his willing accomplice then. Now I drive my car fast too.

These are the memories I stitched into my Strip Quilt, as the snow fell. About sixty hours after I arrived in New Hampshire, we were finally able to dig ourselves out of the subdivision and get on the highway to Boston. I spent the next three days with my father, mostly alone with him, as I had not been since childhood. (The weather was still so bad, and my mother so forlorn that she could not bear to visit him.) We said all the things we needed to say.

I thanked him for being such a good father to me. "Oh, it was easy," he said, his voice thin and reedy, as he panted through his mouth, "because I loved you so much."

I told him I had chosen a sweet-tempered husband, just like him, who loves me enormously. "That's good," he said.

We had never talked to each other like this before. He kept telling me how happy he was that I had come to see him. He kept trying to introduce me to all the nurses: "This is my daughter, the college professor, who came to see me from St. Louis."

"Don't talk, Daddy."

In an effort to keep him from getting too winded from talking, I read to him from one of the car magazines I brought him. I held his right hand in my left one and leaned against the bed, holding the magazine in my other hand. Some of the details I recounted about the latest Maserati are imprinted on my mind: zero to sixty in 5.7 seconds, purchase price of $250,000.

"And a bargain at twice the price," he joked feebly.

His eyes had been closed. I thought he was sleeping.

Bernie almost never asked anything of his daughters, but he had a job for me that day: his car needed to be inspected.

"Take it to my friend John, and tell him you are doing it for me. And Janet, look, don't forget to warm it up real good before you go, or it won't pass the emissions test. While you're at it, take the car on the highway and drive it fast for a couple of miles. It's good for the engine. I won't be driving it for a while."

As I write this, I have the Strip Quilt top (not yet sandwiched) spread out on the floor of my study to give me inspiration. Another memory from childhood wells up, one I hadn't thought of in a long time. It is an image of my father, maybe from 1965 or 1966, changing the oil in the family station wagon. He is lying on the tattered remains of a quilt, one made by his older sister Caroline, I presume. Dirty and oil-stained, it keeps him dry and out of the gutter's grit. Each time he needs it, he takes the quilt carefully out of the trunk and unfolds it onto the street, where it becomes an essential tool in his automotive operation. I am grateful for this image. It proves to me that the love of quilting and the care of cars do come together in an occasional, odd conjunction.

When I finish the quilt, should I give it to my father, to brighten up his hospital room? I don't think so. B. J. and Judith have provided him with more than enough quilts and comforters over the past decade.

This is my Father's Strip Quilt. It will comfort me after he's gone.

MARCH 1994
Patchwork Pictures of Bernie

M y father died last week. He went quickly. "It was like fainting," they told us. Sadness and relief intermingled. We had all seen the demented ninety-two-year-old man who shared my father's hospital room briefly in January. "Nurse! Nurse! Nurse! Nurse!" he cried endlessly, before wetting his bed. We didn't want our dignified and reserved father to become that man.

Judith telephoned me in St. Louis. "Daddy's gone."

I flew to Boston the next day.

We sat in my parents' little apartment, my sisters, my mother, and me. We didn't cry together; we are all intensely private, each in her own way. We discussed funeral and burial arrangements. My father had never been willing to talk about such things or to make any provisions for them. My mother preferred cremation, and we all concurred. The funeral director told us various options for disposal of the "cremains" as they are so archly called now—burial in the ground, placement in a niche at Mount Auburn cemetery, or disposal privately by the family.

"We could take his ashes out to the seashore and cast him into the ocean," Judith said.

"Daddy never liked the water, except from dry land. He got sea sick," I said.

"Well, we can't scatter his ashes from the air either; he hated to fly," B. J. reminded us.

"Do you think we could rent a race car at Indianapolis and have the ashes scattered around the track when the car is going about two hundred miles an hour?" Judith asked.

The giddy laughter was a welcomed relief from our sorrow. Daddy would have grinned at the joke too.

Later that day, Judith and B. J. wanted to divide up his ties. I assume they wanted to make a Memory Quilt out of them. We put them in a big pile on the floor and took turns, each choosing one. After we had done so, I realized I didn't really want any neckties and put my selection back on the floor for them to share. For me his essence was not in his clothes, but in his file cabinet and his top bureau drawer.

I hadn't articulated it to myself before, but once I was at my parents' apartment, I knew I wanted to be the one to go through my father's things. I recognized that my mother wasn't up to it, and I wanted to spare my sisters the extra work—they had both done so much for him in the last three months of his life, when he had been hospitalized. But it was more than that. For me it was also a ritual of saying goodbye. A private, quiet ritual for my private, quiet father.

Late that night after Judith and B. J. had each gone home and my mother had settled down for the night, I began my work. My mother was still so stunned over the loss of her companion of fifty-eight years that she didn't try to meddle or supervise, as she usually does. She left me alone in his corner, his little nest, comprised of his easy chair, television, and reading lamp. His piles of books and automotive magazines. His dishes where nuts and bolts, spark plugs, coins, and cough drops nestled comfortably together, like some odd, personalized Bridge Mix.

I opened his big file cabinet and began systematically to go through it. Anything relating to bank accounts, Medicare, or the current automobile, I would leave for Judith. My job was to discard the extraneous material and to hunt for valued bits of my daddy.

I threw much away: warranties and instruction books for long discarded appliances, brochures on recent car models, personal entry numbers from a decade's worth of Publisher's Clearing House contests, addresses for consumer advocates and senatorial offices, all the bills from his hospital stay of five years ago.

Other files were so intensely evocative of my father that I kept them, secreting them into my suitcase each day without really looking at them carefully or allowing myself to feel their power. That would await my return to my own safe lair, in St. Louis.

There were no surprises. No secret love letters, no cache of sexy magazines, no hidden bank accounts. What I found just deepened and affirmed what I already knew of him: he loved his family and his cars. He enjoyed accounting work, the orderly way that numbers add up and reveal their meaning. He pursued the order and rigor of numbers to a compulsive degree, figuring out interest rates and the average cost of heating and lighting bills. All of these sums were recorded methodically in notebooks, in his neat, Palmer-method script.

I tucked away the drafts of his five-page, hand-written letter to the president of Ford Motor Company, chronicling his complaints about last year's car purchase and the slipshod way repairs were handled by the local dealership. On the last page of the letter he wrote, "I am a Ford man from way back. The first new car I purchased was a 1929 Model A Ford Roadster that cost only $475. Over the years I have purchased twenty-eight cars, and twenty-one of these was a Ford product." He ended with the ultimate threat from "a Ford man from way back": "As soon as the weather gets better, I am going to trade this car in—if I can make a decent deal, maybe on a Toyota."

I found an ancient notebook with the notes he kept of the real-estate commissions of all the men in his father-in-law's real-estate office in the late 1940s. Only because of recent conversations with my mother was I able to deduce that these sums with various initials were his oblique reminders of one of his major disappointments. When my mother's younger brother returned from the Second World War and took over the office that my father had been running, he fired my father. The accounts show that "E. T." had more than twice the commissions that "B. J. B." had in those last two years. Evidence of unfair allocations or of differing capabilities?

I found small, unused appointment books for 1946, 1947, 1948. His name was embossed on the covers in gold leaf. Printed inside were tips for good salesmanship: "Since the war's end there have been far-reaching changes in business. Many returned veterans are on the way up. Many oldsters are on the way out. Aim during 1948 to make one additional contact with up-and-coming men every working day."

The next stage of his career was chronicled in a different folder; it held a few remaining pages of the stationery whose letterhead read "Bernard J. Berlo, Real Estate, 50 Fairbanks St., Fitchburg, Massachusetts." It was like seeing a mirrored image of myself. A folder in one of my file cabinets holds a few pages of stationery from each of the places where I have held visiting appointments in recent years—Dumbarton Oaks, Yale, UCLA. An odd family trait, this keeping of pristine, outdated stationery in manila folders. Will I keep mine until I'm eighty-four? I guess now I will.

I found glossy studio portraits of his older brother Christopher, who had left home to pursue his vocation as a priest in Austria by the time my father was ten. There were reams of paper devoted to car expense records, for every year from 1944 to the present. They chronicled the average cost per gallon of gas, the number of gallons purchased per year, and other cumulative car expenses per year, as well as the average cost per month for running a car. In 1952, the year I was born, his average cost per month was $57.95, with gas at just 29 cents per gallon.

Was it research I was engaged in during those long hours in my father's files? With my background in archaeology and my many years rooting around in libraries, museum storerooms, and archives, I'm expert at rapidly skimming documents and winnowing out what's important. My weekend's research project was in these patches and scraps out of which my father made sense of his history.

Now they were mine to make sense of. What can I deduce from these clues, employing the academic skills that I've used in studying pottery shards and other detritus of lives lived long ago in other civilizations? He valued his place in the order of things, his own biological family, especially his two special siblings, Caroline and Christopher. He kept the holy cards that were printed for their funeral masses. I hadn't realized that his favorite sister had died on his birthday, ten years ago. He kept his Civil Air Patrol card from the Second World War, his Knights of Columbus membership card, not renewed for almost thirty years now. Everywhere I found evidence of his beloved cars, including a list of all twenty-eight he had owned.

The next day I disposed of his clothes with no sentimentality. Two dozen pairs of polyester pants, scores of sport shirts and jackets. My father was always well dressed. Photos from my childhood show him usually in a white shirt and tie. In his retirement he favored sport shirts and nice jackets, picked out by my mother. These clothing and their scents held no power for me. I dispassionately bagged them up and took them down to the St. Vincent de Paul bins at the church. That night I dismantled the contents of his top dresser drawer, where hundreds of little things fit together like a Chinese puzzle, most of them untouched in the twenty years since my parents had moved to this small apartment. Cuff links, a Hopalong Cassidy pocketknife, his brother Chris's army cap, his little brown plastic containers of Indian-head nickels and Mercury-head dimes. I can recall raiding these for candy money when I was small, not knowing that they were special coins. I took these canisters home, to place in my own top drawer.

I threw out the fuses and batteries and nail clippers and store coupons on top of his bureau. I opened his thin wallet, which had come back from the hospital with his other belongings. Just two dollar bills were in it. No need for a thick wad of twenties at the hospital. I looked at his driver's license with its tiny picture—that characteristic big, wide smile that he always wore in photographs.

The business card of his only granddaughter, the tall, prosperous lawyer with an impressive Washington firm. She looks like him and has that characteristic Berlo thatch of thick, shiny dark hair. He was really impressed with her success, earning nearly a six-figure salary, at age of twenty-eight. She also has her grandfather's car sense, shopping around for the best deal on her first new car, a Toyota.

Tucked in the back of the wallet, maybe the most precious item of all, a photo Bernie had carried there for more years than any of us can remember. Taken on his nineteenth birthday, February 10, 1929, it shows my father in his leather jacket and jaunty cap, standing in front of his newly purchased Model A. How to understand this puzzle piece? What did my father see in this image of himself, one that he passed around, at our request, at family get-togethers?

Last winter when I felt so demoralized, so insubstantial, I carried around a little book of snapshots of my quilts, as if to prove to myself that I had value and substance, even though my scholarly self had desiccated to a shriveled husk. I'd sneak a peek at them from time to time. Was this fading sepia photograph an important piece of my aging father's self-image? As an adult man, he lacked many external signs of success: no eminent profession, just a series of hard jobs with long hours; no grand house that had quadrupled in value over the years.

But in 1929, in central Massachusetts, there probably were not too many nineteen-year-olds as flush as Bernie Berlo, who drove around town in a flashy new Model A, paid for in hard-earned cash.

When I got all my secret loot home and began taking it from my suitcase, I knew that I wouldn't hide it away in my own files or in a box labeled "Daddy" to be opened once every few years. I needed to make art out of it.

Yet I was in a quandary, for quilts have been my only medium. I didn't understand how I could incorporate papers and photos and lists and account pages and membership cards into a quilt. Then I began to visualize fine Japanese rice papers, rag papers in different colors, marbled papers. I realized I would make a paper quilt, a collage of two-dimensional items. I envisioned three of them: one for B. J., one for Judith, one for me. I set out directly for the art supply store and bought fifty dollars worth of fine papers, choosing different color schemes for each of us—colors that somehow evoked my father, rich masculine colors. Browns, rusts, and black (with a touch of my own vibrant red) for me. Dark, verdant greens for B. J. Maroons and purples for Judith. I even found hand-spattered papers in shades of maroon, black, and gold that evoked oil stains on a garage floor.

Then, to aid in the stage of playful composition that takes place in any art making, I photocopied lots of the precious photos from his private cache and some from my own as well: school pictures of me as a child that he had kept, a snapshot of him and his three girls in 1968 and again in 1990. Bernie with his brothers and sisters. Photos of his 1953 Buick, his 1942 Plymouth, his 1929 Ford.

I haven't started working on this paper quilt in earnest yet. The component pieces are laid out in my studio, and I finger them sometimes as I walk by. I have cut some of the xeroxed colored-paper photos into small squares with my rotary cutter and used my Bernina to topstitch them with a colorful zigzag stitch to little squares of marbled paper. These four-patches will find their way into my collage memorial to my father.

I don't know how I got to be forty-one years old without death having touched me very closely. This was the first important one for me. I think something elemental goes out of a woman when her father dies.

There is no one but me now who remembers the tricycle rides up Summer Street, in Fitchburg. Daddy tied a rope to my trike and pulled me up the hill. Our destination was the candy store. I got M&Ms.

My father didn't eat candy much. He was an ice cream or pie man. So it seemed like a mysterious gift, that first night when I cleaned out his files and found a bag of M&Ms in the top drawer of the file cabinet. I had been edgy, hungry for chocolate, but my mother had none in the house. I gobbled those little candies down as I picked through the files. Always my favorite treat, I didn't even know that my father ate them.

Perhaps he was saving them for me.

Crazy Ladies and Their Friends

I would like to have known Sallie Jane Edminston Woodward, who lived in North Carolina from 1843 to 1925. Even before the Crazy Quilt mania of the 1880s, her quilts revealed a touch of madness. One, comprised of 5,810 squares and triangles, survives today. The maker celebrated her achievement by embroidering a panel with the triumphant number right in the center of the quilt. The sides of this quilt bulge out, as if the border fabric can barely contain so much energetic pattern.

Sallie Woodward's Crazy Quilt looks much like others of that era, except for the fact that it is bordered with ninety-seven velvet and corduroy embroidered tabs. Oh, and it happens to be reversible to a regular cotton geometric pieced quilt of thirty Barrister's Blocks.[22] She also constructed a singularly extraordinary patchwork dress, reportedly of one thousand pieced blocks. Other extant photos show her in a hat made from a gourd she grew, wearing a cape made of squirrel skins that she had skinned and tanned herself. No doubt a remarkable woman.

It is a pleasure to know at least a little of this woman's offbeat personality. Other "crazy" ladies of the past, we know only by their quilts. African-American quilter Josie Covington made her patchwork masterpiece in Tennessee in 1895, a dazzling, free-form, jazzy index of several dozen patterns.[23]

This was clearly a woman with Attitude.

A decade earlier, Mrs. Samuel Glover Haskins of Granville, Vermont, pieced, appliquéd, and embroidered her forty-two-block Crazy Quilt. Each block has an appliquéd person or animal in the center.[24] I regret that we only know this artistic visionary by her husband's name—not even her own first name has been recorded.

I certainly would like to meet contemporary Oregon quilter Wendy Huhn. Her quilt, *Georgia, Frida, Mary, and Me*, was featured in the Quilt National Exhibition in 1993.[25] While not strictly speaking a Crazy Quilt, this rich textile, which includes pieced and appliquéd fabric, paint, photo transfers, beads, and found objects, reveals, if not a crazy lady, at least one with a wacky frame of mind. The famous women Wendy Huhn chooses as her icons—Georgia O'Keeffe, Frida Kahlo, and the Virgin Mary—certainly are not role models for a prosaic way of life.

This past winter, I helped my friend Kate Kane set her grandmother's Crazy Quilt squares into a black velveteen sashing. Kate finished the embroidery on them, all the while musing about craziness in her own family.

We had bought the velveteen the winter before, when she made her annual Christmas visit to St. Louis. She often stays at my house during these trips, making brief forays into the hornet's nests of family life at her mother's and her father's separate houses. During that Christmas vacation, I was almost emotionally unreachable. I hadn't written anything in six months, I had been quilting like a madwoman for the same amount of time, and the day before I had smashed my husband's flour container and wailed at him in angry despair. I learned later that Bradley had a private talk with Kate about it when they walked the dogs one evening. Circumspect Kate never mentioned a thing. We shopped for fabric together, she made me laugh, and our conversations nibbled, just tentatively, at the edge of my sorrows.

It took Kate the entire twelve months to finish the embroidery on her grandmother's pieces. I held onto the velveteen for safekeeping. Through the long months of working so closely with the squares, she had figured out an arrangement for them. I was the machine seamstress, however. Kate took photos, documenting the process for friendship's archives.

Kate and I have known each other since 1980, when she was a freshman in the first "Women and the Visual Arts" class I taught at the University of Missouri-St. Louis. She still remembers that I wrote on her first paper, an interview with a quilter, "A+. You write very well." Kate later became my research assistant; even a decade later (and three or four research assistants later) she remains unsurpassed: a lightning-quick typist, eagle-eyed proofreader, and writer of clever puns in the margins to make me chortle.

We share a Catholic childhood (and an adulthood of devout apostasy). When she was my research assistant, she would call me "Sister

Mary Compulsiva" when it was time for me to lighten up. When I was sad, she would spontaneously do a dramatic recitation of Dr. Seuss's "Big Green Pants with Nobody inside Them."

Kate is responsible for my having met the love of my life. She called to my attention a fascinating man of whose existence I had been only dimly aware. Her recommendation certainly made me scrutinize him more closely: Kate is gay and seldom looks twice at any man. This was clearly a superior human, of the masculine variety. (Reader, I married him.)

According to Kate, when she was a student, I was her role model.

"You made research look so glamorous," she told me on the eve of getting her own Ph.D., in Media and Communication Studies.

It's hard on the role model to go through a period so intellectually arid that she has nothing to offer her protégé. Then it's time for the tables to be turned. Kate listened and nurtured me. She didn't find me lacking when I grew disillusioned with my profession; it seemed more natural to Kate than perhaps to anyone else who knew me that I should turn to quilting as a means out of my intellectual maze. After all, her formative experience with me was in a class where we spent a number of weeks celebrating quilts as THE great American art. Kate was one of the ringleaders when the class sent a delegation to ask if we could collectively make our own class quilt. It was more an Album Quilt than a Crazy Quilt, with each distinctive square and its maker's name embroidered beneath. No anonymous quilts for us, ardent feminists in 1980!

I've sent Kate some of these "Quilting Lessons" as they've emerged from my pen. Going through a difficult postdissertation depression herself, she was inspired to write some essays back to me.

She wrote about her own family experience with crazy ladies and Crazy Quilts. Her mother was depressed for much of Kate's childhood, leaving her to help raise a large number of younger children. Kate observed,

"Crazy" is a pattern I recognize as familiar/familial. When I was a kid, we had a family "joke" that mom was crazy, something we all just took for granted, something that explained why our family was different from other families. Creative, unpredictable, chaotic—that was our mom, and that was us as a family. I never realized before how calling her crazy allowed her to absorb the dysfunction for the whole group. And how calling her crazy allowed us to be blind to her pain, her anger, her frustration. And how now it makes me feel crazy to recognize my own pain, my own anger, my own frustration, and to separate mine from hers.

As Kate so often does, she astutely gets right to the heart of our shared experience:

Crazy describes the pattern of my work life lately . . . I feel that I am on the edge in many ways—barely performing at work, hardly present in my relationship with my partner. And yet there is also a sense of imminent breakthrough. The crazy pattern has always the potential to re-form, to frame up into something meaningful and interesting.

The crazy pattern has two potentials: one an impulse toward the void; the other a trajectory toward enlightenment. I inhabit them both. The "crazy" part of the metaphor expresses my sense of being psychically drained, as though someone were sticking pins in my soul, sucking out the marrow of my spirit essence. But the "pattern" part restores me, generates creativity, leaves me bubbling over with ideas for my book, for pictures to paint, for essays to write.

I wonder what someone would say about me if they knew only my one enormous Crazy Quilt? In it, mood and pattern decidedly coincide: a lot of sadness and confusion are stitched into that pieced maze, constructed during the worst of my depression, that December of 1992 and January of 1993.

As I do with so many things, I put it aside for nearly a year and came back to finish it up this past spring. I brought it in to show my therapist, as I often do with some quilt project—it is surprising how much light the products of my hands have shed on the circuits of my brain. I told her that it made me edgy to work on it now that I was feeling better. I felt that so much sadness and confusion had been stitched into it. Sadness and confusion that I still did not wholly understand.

"But you recognize how beautiful it is," Dr. Snider said to me more than once. "You do see that, don't you?"

"Well, I think it is visually very interesting, but I wouldn't use the word beautiful."

"It absolutely is beautiful," she insisted. "You have to recognize how you were able to take that pain and confusion and transform it into something beautiful and worthwhile."

It makes me wonder about all those Crazy Quilts at the end of the nineteenth century. They coincided with the rise of the first wave of feminism. Some women held meetings, signed petitions, and formed women's rights organizations. Other women felt an inarticulate longing, a restlessness in their controlled, circumscribed lives. It was premature for most of them to recognize that these feelings were widely shared, that soon they would be marching, that there would be hunger strikes. Women would vote, go to architecture school, get Ph.D.'s. They would break out of their constricted, repetitive patterns.

Crazy, rich, freewheeling, individualistic, unpredictable designs: first they had to work it out in fabric. Only then could they put it into action in their own lives.

APRIL 1994
Back to Unfinished Business

've written a mystery novel, which is two-thirds finished, and an outline and a first chapter for another novel. My scholarly magnum opus sits untouched for nearly two years now.

A dozen quilts in various stages of completion nest in various corners of my studio: Smashed Plates, the Canyon de Chelly Quilt, and several others. In all of these projects, the pattern of work is the same: an initial vision and enthusiasm followed by long weeks or months of exhilarating hard work, followed by a diminution of interest and the turning away to another new endeavor. The unfinished project remains, as a rebuke, on the shelf.

In order not be panicked about this, I have to remind myself of the many things I *have* finished in recent years: some other scholarly articles and reviews, two edited books, a half-dozen quilts. As I think about the quilts that remain unfinished, for the most part they are the ones intended for me. The ones I have easily finished have been gifts for other people. In terms of the writing, sometimes the more distant, abstract, scholarly work gets completed, perhaps because it does not cost very much to do so. The more personal, self-revelatory work, that which tries to find new avenues for combining scholarship and feeling, gets put aside.

So is there a pattern in both the writing and the quilting? Do the important projects, in which some personal issues are being explored and worked out, remain unfinished?

Spring is blossoming, and the academic year is coming to a close. Summer stretches out in front of me, filled with weeks and weeks worth of time. This is the season when traditionally I have been at my most productive and prolific as a scholar. Perhaps this year it would be good to set the goal of finishing some projects.

Since I seem to respond so strongly to palpable, material things, I probably should start with quilts and practice the art of finishing. Perhaps this would give me the courage and the conviction to finish some important writing projects as well.

"What is it about finishing?" the Dr. Snider in my head asks.

An unfinished project can't be judged yet. Its perfection or imperfection remains a relative thing, in flux. Perhaps it is at its most perfect while still in pieces, where it has not yet been measured against that ideal image in the mind's eye. Or perhaps its current imperfections are not worrisome, for one has ambitious plans to make it perfect in the next stage.

I put my pen down, look out the window at the trees in bud, and then focus again on that last paragraph. What leaps out as the important, recurring word? Perfection.

A sticky word, especially for us overachievers. We always expect perfection of ourselves. Too bad. For it means we are destined to be disappointed every single time. There is no perfection here.

I consider myself a superb proofreader and copyeditor. Every book or article I have written has been checked and rechecked for spelling errors, typographical errors, and clumsy phrases. There are, of course, editors who get paid for such work, but I always recheck it myself as well. Yet it never fails: when the pristine, unopened book or periodical arrives in the mail, I am proud to see my name and my words typeset on fine paper, bound, and stamped with an ISBN number and publication date. I always find an error within the first few minutes. It protects against hubris, I guess.

In many cultures, artists (particularly women artists, now that I think about it) deal with this trap of "perfection" by doing with deliberation what the rest of us do inadvertently, just by being fallible humans. They intentionally introduce an error or an irregularity into the pattern. Navajo blanket weavers, Islamic carpet weavers, Pomo basket makers, and Pueblo pottery painters customarily do something to interrupt the flow of expected pattern. If weaving a textile with a predominantly white center and a red, enframing border, a Navajo weaver might deliberately take one white weft thread and run it out to the selvage to provide a pattern break.

A Pomo artist who is twining a complex, repetitive design around her beautiful, symmetrical basket will introduce an irregularity in the patterning. This is called a *dau*. It functions as a signature—for each weaver's *dau* is idiosyncratic—as well as a visual reminder that perfection is not to be achieved.

African-American quilters often introduce irregularities into a repeating pattern. A quilt of twelve Bear's Paw blocks might have one block in which the claw-point triangles are reversed, or perhaps one whole quarter block will be inset upside down. To the outsider's eye, trained to expect rigor and precision in a repeating quilt pattern, it might look like carelessness, but it is a deliberate act.

Fallibility, irregularity, ambiguity, asymmetry. All fall short of "perfection." All exist in nature and art for a reason. They introduce something interesting, some conflict, something for the eye or the mind to linger on.

So let's discard this straightjacket of perfectionism. It isn't attainable anyway. It's like trying to be taller. Neither wishing nor striving (nor procrastinating!) will make it so.

As I embark upon my spring resolution of finishing up some of the unfinished business in my studio, my first task should be to finish the big green Serendipity Quilt that I worked on, not this past winter, but the winter before: the first winter of my discontent. I happened upon the term Serendipity Quilt as I thought about the process of designing it, which was really no structured process at all.

I scorned the precise and sought the fortuitous.

I wonder now if perhaps an underlying issue was trust. Trusting myself to know the way out of the impasse. Trusting my intuitive sense of design. Not overdetermining the pattern. Letting it happen.

"Trust. Trust that you'll find what you need. Trust that what has been put down will be picked up. Trust yourself to finish," I mutter out loud, as if to make the words stick.

I thought that finishing the Serendipity Quilt would be good practice for my writing. But I found it upsetting to work on the machine quilting and binding. It uncovered the waves of unhappiness that had engulfed me as I sewed the previous winter. I found that I hadn't yet fully figured out what all the pain and scholarly amnesia had been about. But a lot of those feelings had been stitched into the "Serendipity in Green" Quilt.

No matter what kind of quilts I am working on, structured or free-form, or what kind of academic work I'm doing, every few weeks I need to take a day out for small bursts of serendipity: Serendipity Place Mats. These can be finished in a day. For me, they seem to work out life's larger issues in a miniature arena.

Quilting lessons in miniature: reminders to trust in the process, rely on intuition, and a pattern will emerge.

Kate Anderson, a painter, delights in these place mats.

"I just love them!" she cries, laughing happily at my color collisions and the funky machine embroidery I do on the seams with my ancient Singer Touch-and-Sew.

"They're just darling little abstract paintings! Don't bind them. You don't know it yet, but they're not really place mats. I want to see them matted and framed, on the wall," she says decisively, in a way that makes me understand how she is so successful in her day job as an art-gallery director.

"I've got a client who will just adore these. I'm going to bring her to your studio and tell her just how great they'll look on the walls of her office."

Perhaps I should hang them on the walls. Not for aesthetic reasons and certainly not for the benefit of a stranger, but for reasons of my own mental health. They truly are my little quilting lessons, testimony to the power of serendipity.

As this spring emerged, my secret hope was that I could wrap up all my unfinished business by summer's end: finish all the unfinished quilts, finish this book, finish therapy. Wrap it all up in a tidy package.

Life's not that neat and easy. This book will end sometime soon, but quilters always have unfinished work. Eventually, one can reach a reasonable stopping point in long-term therapy, but the messy business of piecing life's patterns together doesn't end, until life itself is finished.

MAY 1994
Working My Stint

T he last few weeks, in my push to "finish up," I've been exemplary about consistently completing a stint of machine quilting, every day, on something that has been sandwiched but not yet finished. Today I worked on the Father Quilt. This stitching framed my work day like parentheses: twenty minutes at 8 A.M., another twenty at 4 P.M.

I don't really enjoy the process of machine quilting. The ungainly bulk of the work, the precision of "stitching in the ditch," and the vigilance required not to stitch one-thirty-secondth of an inch outside the ditch conspire to give me a giant crimp between my shoulder blades within a few minutes of starting. For that reason, I try to spend no more than a half-hour at a time on it. I also measure out similar stints when I am hand hemming the binding of a quilt. Through these steady increments, the tedious tasks are completed.

This stint-work is, of course, a time-honored tradition in quilting. Many older quilters recall the discipline imposed on them as children who had to "sew a stint" before they were free to play. Jessie Carter related her mother's childhood memory of sewing one perfect yard of seam per day. Any imperfections and the entire stint would be ripped out and resewn.[26]

Quilters' girlhood diaries record this practice as well. Caroline Richards says, "I am sewing a sheet over and over for Grandmother, and she puts a pin in to show me my stint before I can go out and play." Helen Doyle writes, "Every day I must sew one square of nine blocks before I am free to play."[27]

Curiously, I have seldom tried to approach my academic work in this fashion. Instead I get fierce and high-handed: "You *must* sit down at that desk at 8 A.M. tomorrow, and you *will* not get up until you've written, typed, and edited five polished pages!"

Against this inner tyrant, my rebellion has been total, these last twenty-two months. I have written very little and have abandoned the Macintosh in favor of the Bernina. But recently, some part of me has been reaching slyly toward the academic world that I had abandoned. I've written some grant proposals in support of future academic work and travels. To my surprise, they all have been funded. I have the prospect of a number of new research projects ahead of me starting this summer, but first I must bring some others to completion.

As I begin this season of Finishing Up, it strikes me that the way to approach the writing of one dreaded article (which is currently nine months overdue at the editor's desk) is through the old-fashioned quilter's device of the stint. What would happen if I were to tell myself that tomorrow my first stint would be one half-hour at the writing desk? It's so easy—and so self-defeating—to feel that thirty minutes is an insignificant amount of time. What could possibly be accomplished?

A few years ago, when I was an administrator at a research center for a year, I very much admired one elderly Oxford professor of exemplary research habits, who had confided, "I work at my desk all morning, and when I begin to feel hungry for my dinner, I get up and stretch my legs. Then I persist for another quarter-hour." I suspect that it was the steady pile-up of these quarter-hours, over more than half a century, that earned him his eminence.

Of course, the secret to such stints is that on at least a few special days, one's shoulders won't ache, one's stomach won't rumble, one's ideas won't clog; indeed, before the head is raised from the work, a good deal more than one, or two, or three quarter-hours will have passed.

Even if every quarter-hour is hard won, it's still worth it.

MAY 1994
Hard at Play

D olphins, which are the smallest whales, spend three-quarters of their lives in play. What does it mean when one of the oldest brains on the planet, the whale's, devotes so much time to play? Is there a lesson here for us?"[28] These words, in a book of nature essays, stopped me in my tracks.

In 1992, having lost a sense of joy and playfulness in my academic work, I seized upon quilt making as an arena for play and visual delight. It has never disappointed me. The accumulation of variable blocks to be sewn into a larger pattern—this is work done with a light heart.

These essays too usually are pleasurable and playful in their execution. I often sit down not knowing exactly what I want to construct, what word designs will lie down companionably, or where a pattern of thought will take me.

The Museum of the American Quilter recently featured an exhibit that exemplified the playfulness of the best contemporary art quilts. "Double Wedding Ring: New Quilts from Old Favorites" showcased eighteen prize-winning entries from hundreds submitted. The object of the juried contest was to take one of the best-known and most

easily recognized patterns and, well, *play* with it. The first place win-
ner, "Log Cabin Double Wedding Ring," by Keiko Goke of Japan, is a
unique and exuberant interpretation of this classic design.[29] The artist
zoomed in on just a couple interlocking rings of the pattern, made
them asymmetrical, and constructed them out of slightly crooked and
imprecise Log Cabin blocks. A few small Log Cabin squares appliquéd
to the surface seem to fly through the air.

Playfulness allows us to suspend normal rules of comportment and
behavior, be it abstract, linear thinking or gridded, symmetrical quilt
patterns. Quirkiness and originality are prized in the playful mind.

I would like to be more childlike (that is: free, unconstrained by
overintellectualization), yet paradoxically, what I struggle with is
being too childish—undisciplined in my work habits, petulant about
some of the daily tedium of seeing projects through, savoring the
excitement of starting something then losing interest. How to get
around this essential paradox: to be playful but in a disciplined, productive way?

I do have lots of practice, for this is exactly what most of my quilts
are about. But I'm still a beginner at transferring this aptitude for
disciplined play to my academic pursuits.

Some of it relates to the issue of finishing, as I've explored elsewhere in these pages. For me, starting is the most playful, exuberant
part of any enterprise, be it quilt making, creative writing, or scholarship. All those fabric possibilities to *juggle*! All those ideas and plots to
scribble down! All those new realms of knowledge to *devour*! Even the
verbs evoke energy and play: juggle, scribble, devour.

Midstream in the process, the action becomes more staid; the quilt
must be sandwiched, the paragraphs edited, the footnotes written. So
much easier to procrastinate, set the project aside, and embark on the
carefree beginning of some new project.

I am far from solving this problem, but it is one that I will grapple
with all summer long as I try to finish up some quilts, this book, and
some art historical articles. How to keep my sense of purposeful play
while maintaining the discipline that is necessary to bring projects to
closure?

I began this book after a twelve-month scholarly silence, a deafening silence, in which I abandoned all academic work in favor of quilt making. This was a very painful time, in terms of the writer's block I was experiencing. Paradoxically, it was also a time of great artistic creativity.

From this total immersion in patchwork quilts, I emerged transformed as a writer. Part of the very hard lesson I needed to learn was how to make my work more like play and how to enjoy my immersion in the play of it rather than to get caught up in the relentless pursuit of the finish line. My unconscious chose to shut down the writing sweatshop entirely, in order that these lessons might take place. As my therapist commented during one of my first consultations (when, after eight months, my concern about my writer's block threatened to spiral out of control), there is certainly no more effective way of getting the attention of a writer than to shut off the writing!

So the writing ceased, and the quilt making commenced. I experienced the cutting and piecing of fabric as the most delightfully absorbing play I had experienced since I was ten years old. And like a small child, I played really hard! For, as child psychiatrists observe, small children's play is hard work. They throw themselves into it, physically and psychically. This is the job of childhood, to be hard at play.

For a while, I thought I was just taking a break from my work. The "break" went on for months. In my professional world, I was rather embarrassed about it; no one except my husband really knew how completely I had broken from my previous, exemplary habits as a scholar. A few colleagues knew I was making quilts, but they surely didn't know that on those days when I was not teaching at the university I was quilting all day. Even my two closest friends, both art historians like myself, had no idea how much my world had been transformed.

When I tried to hint at it, they said, "Of course! Take a break! You deserve it. You've published enough. Enjoy yourself!"

Not bad advice, but it seemed beside the point. I was not "taking" a break. Rather, it seemed that everything in my carefully ordered life had been broken—smashed to pieces.

In college I read a book about the great Swiss psychologist Carl Jung. He described how he went about understanding the process of children's play activities. He did not (as research psychologists would do today) set up studies to analyze children's behavior or take notes while he observed them through a two-way mirror. No. He played. He abandoned all his work responsibilities and played for an entire year.

While I did not consciously set out to change my life, spending more than a year and a half at play so far (both making quilts and then writing about it) achieved precisely that.

My own work (whether scholarly or artistic, and what is this simpleminded dichotomy, anyway?) is becoming more like the art I was looking at and writing about in the book I abandoned when Quilt Madness took over: freewheeling, inventive, open to experimentation, playful.

My prior scholarly life, in contrast, had become the kind of quilt that I am constitutionally unable to make: the kind where you choose a pattern block, make one, assess it, and then make twenty-nine more just like it. Although I admire these works visually, the act of making them is too rigid, controlled, and overdetermined for me.

Too much like work. I prefer to play.

Perhaps I had half-understood these issues intellectually, but now my long apprenticeship in the *practice* of women's art has made me learn them viscerally and kinesthetically. I've moved away from the model of scholarship involving long, consecutive hours at my desk. I've rearranged a corner of the living room to make it more hospitable for writing. I write for thirty minutes on the couch or at a small table I moved in front of the window to overlook my perennial garden. I type out fragments, paragraphs, ideas on different pieces of paper and arrange them in patterns on the floor, much as I arrange the different but related blocks of my quilts.

My work has become physically active rather than immobile. Not sitting in one chair at the computer, or hunched over books or a notepad for hours on end. Instead, I'm much more likely to work in bits and pieces. Quilting practice has become my model: moving from standing at the high cutting table, where I use my rotary cutter to make strips, to sitting at the sewing table to flash-feed two dozen stacked triangles through the sewing machine, to standing up at the taller table again to press the squares, to bending down to the floor where the quilt-in-progress takes shape. I've found in these actions a simple rhythm and grace of movement, like Tai Chi or yoga. Its casualness suits me, for I am not temperamentally inclined to jogging tracks or workout equipment.

My Serendipity Quilt work involves multiple patterns held in the eye simultaneously. This is very different from the straightforward, linear unfolding of a narrative scholarly argument. I suspect I'll never fully return to the paralysis of that scholarly model again. I've outgrown it. I've grown into the age of constant playfulness.

Work suggests rigorous, linear, orderly patterning.

Play shows us how to break free of those constraints, out of linearity and rules, and into a coherent, yet freer whole.

JUNE 1994

An Amish Nine-Patch

L ast week I flew to Boston to pick up my father's car, which my mother had given to me, and drive it back to St. Louis. Not looking forward to the tedium of twelve hundred highway miles, I was thrilled when B. J. offered to accompany me on the trip. I picked her up in New Hampshire Friday morning of Memorial Day weekend, and we began our journey west. The first day we drove from Auburn, New Hampshire, to Wilkes-Barre, Pennsylvania, a distance of nearly 450 miles. Optimistic about having traveled so far, we decided to detour the next day through Lancaster County, Pennsylvania. Neither of us had ever traveled through Amish country, so a little taste of it would be our diversion on the long ride west.

It is uncharacteristic for me simply to drop in on a tourist destination. I typically wage the definitive campaign: assemble all maps, consult all guidebooks, plan an exemplary tour. But here we were simply relying on serendipity. We managed to pick up a Lancaster County map, and we both knew that the infamously named town of

Intercourse was in the heart of Amish country. B. J. said, "Let's head there first and move outwards from there."

Gradually the suburban sprawl waned, and we entered a verdant valley of farms. Not all of them were Amish-owned, but we began to see signs: a horse-drawn buggy, a man plowing with a horse team.

Driving into Intercourse, I felt as if we had fallen though the Amish looking glass into a touristic horror show. Chartered busses disgorged hordes in Bermuda shorts from New York, Baltimore, and Philadelphia. They poured into Fudge Shoppes, Ice Cream Shoppes, and so-called Folk Art Shoppes selling stinking bowls of potpourri and stenciled chalkboards proclaiming "Welcome Friends." Nothing genuine, authentic, or heartfelt in the place. To my eyes, everything was ersatz, saccharine, fraudulent. I rush to my thesaurus to pile up the synonyms, for three are not enough: adulterated, bogus, counterfeit, fake, fictitious, illegitimate, perfidious, sham.

In these situations, my pedantic mind goes into overdrive. Under my breath, I muttered half-remembered fragments from sociologist Dean MacCannell's classic book on twentieth-century tourism: "the middle class systematically scavenges the earth for new experiences to be woven into a collective, touristic version of other peoples and other places," and "modern society is vulnerable to overthrow from within through nostalgia."[30]

Not being a crabby cultural critic like me, B. J. was content to take it all in, from horse plow to Fudge Shoppe. Her sunny disposition found something of value in every part of it: the juxtaposition of two colors or patterns in an otherwise hideous quilted scrapbook cover, the little cookie-cutter patterns of saw and hammer that could be used as an idea for an appliqué quilt. I, on the other hand, wanted to run screaming from the scene.

B. J. shepherded me to Zook's Dry Goods Store, not a touristic simulacrum but a verifiably Amish-run establishment: no credit cards, closed on Sunday, and not a whiff of potpourri around. It was quilter's heaven and an oasis from the cross-cultural cacophony outside its doors. This was the one place in the bustling tourist mecca of Intercourse where I did not feel like a hideous interloper. Here, fabric served as the Esperanto among women of disparate races, social classes, and religions. Amish women, Mennonite women, and "English" women (the rest of us) mingled amiably there. The store held something of value for all. Black serge and navy polyester for Amish women to sew into clothing for their men. Modestly sprigged cottons and Dacrons for the Mennonite women. And a wide variety of splendid cotton prints for the rest of us. Notably, these were not priced at the customary $6.98 and $7.98 that Hoffmann and Ginny Beyer prints command in most fabric shops. $4.95 and $5.25 apparently provided ample profit for the Zook family.

As she hefted the big bolts of cloth, the young Amish woman who cut my fabric at Zook's Dry Goods could comment knowledgeably on which colorful Hoffmann or Alexander Henry prints came in different hues. Yet her handmade blouse, of plain lavender polyester, was fastened with straight pins, and her limp hair was concealed beneath a gauzy cap.

Amish country was qualitatively different from many destinations I have visited as a scholar or a tourist. Though the people and their way of life were the focus of tourists' curiosity, these objects of our attention looked back in an extraordinary way. Their gaze was cordial, egalitarian, but essentially disinterested. In some parts of the developing world where I've traveled, I've been embarrassed by the sense that those who were my hosts—the Maya in highland Guatemala, for example, or Indians on various reservations in the United States— were also embarrassed by my presence. Perhaps too long inculcated by propaganda about Western superiority, they seemed apologetic about their poverty or their "quaintness." In Amish country, in contrast, I sensed that these people were confident in the superiority of their own culture and remarkably uninterested in mine.

After leaving Zook's with our precious yards of fabric to remind us of our Amish visit, we stopped to examine quilts for sale. Made in traditional Amish colors and designs, they were high priced and well crafted. It was clear, as we drove to different shops and barn sales, that women's needlework garnered a significant amount of income for the communities. But curiously, the quilts themselves are not what fed my mind's eye as I traversed the countryside, nor are they what nourish me now. Instead, I see little mental snapshots that resolve into colors and patterns that will be incorporated into my own future quilts.

The quart bottles of sweet and sour chowchow for sale on simple tables set up along country lanes: a riotous mix of snap bean, sweet pepper, limas, celery, and carrot, looking homely and comforting in their glass quart jars.

The subtle variants of brown in the land and the horses: chestnut, roan, beige, chocolate. The stalwart, chunky plow horses of light brown contrasted with the sleek dark chestnut horses that pranced merrily as they pulled their gray carriages. (In the one concession to modernity, reflector lights were affixed to the backs of these carriages, to give them some small defense against vehicles powered by much stronger horsepower than theirs.)

The laundry hanging out to dry behind the dozens of farm houses we passed on that sunny seventy-five degree day: mostly white and black, syncopated by an occasional flash of brilliant magenta of a woman's blouse.

Yet it is my first image of Amish country that stays most vivid: we drove around a corner on a country road and passed by a field. From behind, I saw a teen-aged Amish girl plowing the field. (Even as I write that, it sounds wrong. The concept of teenager is alien to Amish culture. I saw little girls of ten, playing, giggling, and running, and I saw young women of thirteen, who calmly worked beside adult women, with the same capable demeanor.) Correction: I saw a strong, young Amish woman standing astride a plow. She expertly handled a team of five sturdy horses. Even standing on the plow, her head barely reached above their rumps. The vivid blue of her dress sang out against the dark brown clods of earth she plowed and the dun-colored work horses.

Visiting the Amish, even just for one afternoon, leads me back to re-visit Sue Bender's marvelous book, *Plain and Simple*.[31] In it, she recounts her irrational desire to live with an Amish family (irrational because, as an iconoclastic artist living in Berkeley, she knows she won't fit in). Her guiding metaphor throughout the book is the simple Nine-Patch. She dyes fabric, stains it with coffee and tea, and cuts it into small squares, rearranging them according to shade and pattern. This simple design becomes her structure for working out artistic problems and problems of daily life too. Like a haiku, a Nine-Patch is deceptively simple in its structure. It takes rigorous paring down to make it work. Like a haiku, when well done, it achieves poetic elegance.

This requires filtering out all the confusion and extraneous detail. Bender finds that by working with a Nine-Patch, meditatively and repetitively, life's cacophony is extinguished. So too, on the outskirts of Intercourse, Pennsylvania, the simple flash of a blue skirt against the brown of horse and field drowns out tourism's dissonant clamor.

Only the simple Amish image remains.

Chowchow: Recipe for a Sixteen-Patch

It's a scrap quilt in a bottle, really.

Bits of red pepper, yellow wax beans, maroon kidney beans, light green lima beans, darker pole beans, orange carrot medallions, and crescents of watermelon rind all mixed together in a sugary vinegar. Gleaming glass jars reveal all of these bits and pieces, and the mouth waters just looking at it.

The novelist Alice Walker has written about glass canning jars, filled to the brim with the wonderful colors of the harvest, forming the only artistic decorations (other than quilts) in the homes of southern Black women. It is the same for Amish women—the only ornaments are those of practical function, proclaiming industry and frugality.

As I wrote about the Amish, I was moved to go down to the kitchen and dip a spoon into the quart jar of chowchow that I carried home from a farm stand near Bird-in-Hand, Pennsylvania. The wedges of watermelon rind are tinged with red that fades into yellow green. My favored yellows nestle next to pale celery greens.

Should I try to translate these into fabric—a sweet-and-sour chow-chow quilt? Too ambitious for today, in a month when I need to finish up too many things and prepare for an upcoming research trip to Alaska. But life can't be all paperwork, itineraries, car registration forms, footnotes, and bibliographic index cards. Perhaps this after-noon I could offer myself an hour of playing with fabric squares. A little cache of chowchow squares to harvest later in the season, to remind me of an Amish morning in May.

Dog Patch

M y beloved Floop died in her sleep the other night. Floop was a bloodhound, with the most beautiful chestnut and black fur, and the most exceptionally long and sensuous ears. She was lying so still, in her customary corner of the bedroom. Always an ardent food hound, clearly something was wrong when she didn't get up with me and her sidekick, the Great Dane pup, for a 6 A.M. breakfast.

"Floopy," I called, knowing enough not to invade her space—she was fierce about her privacy when resting.

"Floop? Don't you want your dog food?" Those two magic words to enliven a hound's soul.

"Dog food, Floopy!"

She was too still. I touched her paw. It was cold. She looked so peaceful—just sleeping. But she was dead.

In preparation for my research trip to Alaska next week, I've been reading a lot of anthropological studies about Eskimos. According to their traditional belief, all animals, not just the human ones, have souls. All of us are sentient beings. Dog owners, of course, know the truth of this.

Traditional Alaskan Eskimo hunters honored the souls of the sea mammals they killed. They saved and dried each animal's bladder for use in the winter festival, when the bladders were inflated and cast back into the sea. I picture a raft of parchment balloons, taking back to the undersea world the news that the human people love and respect the seal people and are grateful that the animals let themselves be taken. The return of the bladders ensures the continuation of future generations, for it casts back the animal's soul, to be recycled.

Floop was a stray dog. By the worn-down state of her nails and the ribs we could see through the thick brown fur, she had covered a lot of miles that February before she walked into our lives. No one claimed her at the animal shelter, so she was ours. Or perhaps I should say she let herself be taken by us.

She was a complicated beast. Not simple in her urge to please, like most dogs I've known, she could be churlish and cranky. She was willing to grant my right to be top dog, but she vied for many months with Bradley for second place. Only reluctantly did she cede superiority to him, and only after a dozen battles of which he, rather than she, bears the scars. She was fierce with strangers who rang the doorbell and held a particular animosity for letter carriers and UPS drivers. Yet thunder and lightning sent her into our laps or into my closet, where I soon learned to clear the floor of shoes and other detritus and make a "thunder bed" for Floop.

So this week, when my thoughts are supposed to be on scholarly reading and packing my suitcase with a wardrobe that will take me from St. Louis's ninety degrees to Fairbanks's morning lows of forty-two, instead I sit in my study and think of Floop. She was a great companion to my scholarly work, just as her predecessor, Nanaimo, the St. Bernard, had been. During our first two years together, Floop would accompany me to my third-floor retreat every day. After breakfast and dog walk and Bradley's departure, she'd stand in the front hall like some scholarly Enforcer, waiting for the cue from me. The command "third floor!" would send her rocketing up two flights of stairs.

In my study she would doze, changing position every hour or two. She seldom bothered me at my desk, for we seemed to have a mutual understanding about autonomy, concentration, and personal space. She didn't sleep at my feet, like my St. Bernard had, in another third-floor study in another house. Floop found places of her own choosing, often following the patch of sun as it moved across my south-facing window. We would go downstairs every hour or two for biscuits or tea, each according to her own needs. Perhaps we'd sit on the deck for fifteen minutes, then go back upstairs to our work. Her internal food alarm would sound by 4 P.M. Only then would she come over and slide her snout under my left arm, again and again, and motion for me to get up. If I ignored her, she would make a series of compelling little canine noises until I allowed her to lead me downstairs. It made me understand more vividly the meaning of the adverb *doggedly*.

When quilt making took over my heart and my study nearly two years ago, I'm sorry to say that Floop was banished from the third floor. The few times I had her up there with me as I worked, she would perceive the various lengths of fabric arrayed on the floor or the quilt blocks laid out for joining as an invitation to curl up on them. So I have no recent, vivid image of Floop upstairs with me. The first year of quilting, Floop would sleep in the living room alone; the second year she had the companionship of Russell, her Great Dane pal, for another needy dog had wandered into our lives.

The night after she died, I woke up in tears from a nightmare. In the dream, I went upstairs to my study, and she was lying on the carpet, not sleeping but dead, in the exact position in which I had, in reality, found her body. I went downstairs and came up again, and her lifeless body had mysteriously moved. It was draped over the rolling file cart that contains some of the files for my neglected book. I was horrified and turned to go downstairs again. Russell's body lay limp on the stairs, like a stuffed animal. He, too, was dead. I went back to the bedroom. Suddenly it was the middle of the night, and Bradley was making a trip to the FedEx office. I was filled with dread at the possibility of his being kidnapped or shot in that dangerous neighborhood so late at night.

The dream reveals how profound my fear of loss and abandonment must be. The animals are dead, Bradley is endangered, and Floop's body is draped over the files of my "dead" book. Significantly, the one thing dear to me that does not figure in the dream is quilting. I guess I have no fear of losing my love of fabric and the consolation this work brings me.

Yesterday and the day before, I was too sad to read and too sad to pack. I have never yet been too sad to sew. I sat in my study and sewed some place mats and thought about Floop. Sometimes my eyes were blurred by tears, but the feed dogs (feed dogs!) still pulled the fabric through the machine.

When I called Bradley to come and see if our Floopy were really dead, he knelt in front of her and put his head down on her chest. Had she been alive, it would have been a scary thing to do, tantamount to braving the lion in her den. She lay in her favorite sleeping nook in the bedroom, a little three feet by four feet passageway in front of my closet.

"She has no heartbeat," he said simply and put his head down on her again. "Oh, my sweet pup."

The lioness did not stir.

To move her would take both of us, for she weighed ninety pounds. I had the urge to wrap her in some comforting quilt. In the linen closet I found one of Bradley's old favorites, a duvet cover we hadn't used in years, one his sisters had made for him when he went away to school.

"Can Floop have this?" I asked.

"Of course," Bradley said. "It's patterned with animals. It's the right one."

We used it as a sling to carry her downstairs and out to the car trunk. Bradley left her wrapped in it at the vet. I like to think of her being cremated in it. The urge to wrap the dead in some special cloth is a primal one, I think. Archaeologists find mortuary textiles everywhere that humans have lived.

And the urge for the living to commemorate the dead with textiles is perhaps a primal one as well. I called B. J. to tell her that Floop was gone; they had been special pals.

"Oh, honey," she said. "Take the time to really think about her and mourn. Maybe you could make a little wall hanging with all her lovely browns and blacks."

And so I shall.

Her long sleek ears will have to be represented somehow. And her exceptional fondness for rawhide chews. Perhaps it will be a mixed-media work: fabric and raw hide. Months ago I bought some white fabric with small black dog paws on it. That will be the background. I will see if, as I predicted a year ago in "Loss," quilting can forge a path through sorrow and the loss of a beloved one.

"Third floor, Floop!" Let's go quilt.

Robbing Peter to Pay Paul

R obbing Peter to Pay Paul is the name of a traditional quilt block pattern. It involves piecing a block in two colors, alternating the placement of those colors. It gives the appearance of removing a dark piece from one block and setting it down in the light block next door, and vice versa. Some quilters assume that this memorable name is biblical in origin, but apparently it derives from British history, when in the sixteenth century, King Edward VI ordered St. Peter's church in Westminster to sell some of its land in order to pay for the repair of St. Paul's in London.[32]

Describing this quilt pattern in art historical terms, I would mention the use of positive and negative space, for the large repeating pattern is simply the juxtaposition of the same geometric shapes in alternating color patterns. To a psychoanalyst, the term that would most readily come to mind would be displacement. For one color displaces another within the alternating squares.

I have never made this quilt pattern, because I shy away from curved seams. Yet I like its strong, bold look, and I think of the phrase Robbing Peter to Pay Paul often as I quilt or write about quilts. I think of it in terms of my own displacement activity—taking time, energy, and resources from one project and devoting it to another.

I started this small essay a year ago—precisely fifty-one weeks, according to the date on the computer file. Got two-thirds of it sketched out. Couldn't quite pull it together. Yet today, when it is imperative that I finish another article that is more than eleven months overdue, instead I attend to this essay. Why? This is certainly a displacement of intellectual energy—the good clearheaded morning energy that I prize so much.

Maybe it's time to realize that this process really is just Robbing Janet to Pay Janet. In other words, it is all work that needs to be done. Perhaps the order in which it is accomplished is less important than I think.

In The Quilters, one Texas needlewoman says "If I have a color scheme, I can have my housework done and be quilting by 7 A.M."[33] It's

7:10 A.M. as I write this. I've had breakfast, walked the dog, and read the *New York Times*. I had intended to sit right down at the computer and work on the scholarly article that has been nagging at me. The idea fills me with anxiety. I've avoided it for months, replicating on a small scale my problems with The Book. I don't want to grapple with it.

"Grapple" with it? My word choice derives from wrestling or football—dangerous, physically arduous sports. Why is that? I never think about my quilting in that way, only my scholarly work.

"Robbing Peter to Pay Paul" could be the theme song of my scholarly life. I have always had several projects going at once. If I hit a snag or an impasse on one, I can take up another. This has proved ultimately to be far more productive than other common displacement activities like watching TV, shopping, or reading a novel. If it's not a day when I can generate new ideas for an exhibition I'm working on, perhaps the time is right to finish all those pedantic footnotes for my essay in *Art Bulletin*. If my frame of mind isn't right to do the exacting piecing on the Sisters' Quilt, perhaps I can finish up the mindless hand binding of the Father Quilt.

Most of us castigate ourselves far too often. We use a lot of "shoulds" and "musts." Instead of worrying that I SHOULD be cleaning the house now or I SHOULD be writing my article now, or I MUST correct these papers before I do anything else, it might be more empowering to step back and look at the larger picture. As long as the housework USUALLY gets done, and the articles EVENTUALLY get written, and the papers GENERALLY get graded in a reasonable amount of time, it's okay to Rob Peter to Pay Paul. In fact, sometimes it is precisely the pattern required. For twenty-three months (but who's counting!), I've been Robbing Peter to Pay Paul as I make quilts rather than write The Book. Now I can finally begin to stand back enough to see the larger pattern that emerges from this period. It's been quite a complex one: many quilts completed and even more begun, over two dozen "Quilting Lesson" essays that are shaping up into a book, the winning of some grants for future scholarly endeavors. All in all, the artistic quadrant of my life is quite rich, and the scholarly one is, tentatively, beginning to bloom again.

It is important to take pleasure in the overall pattern, rather than focusing on the shortcomings of any one square. When I get angry at myself for "squandering" my time and energy on one project when there is another that the boss in my head thinks is more pressing, I need to stop looking at the one quilt block (this afternoon, my project at hand, or even this season) and look at the whole quilt (the entire day, my work as a whole, my life).

A good rule of thumb, both in quilt design and in the design for living: a strong, complex, geometric design is achieved by repeated alternations, not simple repetition of the same thing.

JULY 1994
Dreaming of Double Woman

A year ago, in "Unfinished Business," I wrote of my book on Native American women's art: "Perhaps, like an unfinished quilt, I should pack it away, secure in the knowledge that the time will come to finally piece it together."

I still haven't boxed it up, but increasingly, I'm thinking about of the importance of that gesture. The scholarly side of my study is littered with evidence of the book: big, sloppy stacks of files and Xeroxes, towering heaps of research volumes, memos about photos ordered from museums, various drafts marked with editorial comments by me, by Aldona, and by Ruth.

My therapist chuckled, months ago, when she heard the title of the book.

"*Dreaming of Double Woman?*" she said. "That's you. Isn't that what our conversations are about? The doubleness of your life? Scholar-artist. Our work is to integrate those sides, make them whole."

The title of my book stems from one of the key myths of Lakota culture. The spirit figure called Double Woman is so named because she has two personae—beautiful and holy as well as ugly and dangerous. Notably, Lakota women who "dream of Double Woman" excel at the arts of quillwork and beadwork, for it was she who taught these arts to womankind in the distant past. If one dreams too much of Double Woman, Lakota women say, one's life may become unbalanced, devoted too much to art and not enough to family, community, and the rhythms of daily life.

This cautionary tale serves equally as an enabling myth, for it spiritually sanctions the work of those women who immerse themselves in artistic production to the exclusion of other things.[34] There are few enough myths in any culture that say it's okay for a woman to make art and neglect her domestic duties—we should pay attention when we find one!

One of the most poignant myths in the classical tradition concerns Demeter and Persephone. Demeter, the grain mother, becomes so distraught over the abduction of her daughter into the underworld that she refuses to sit with the other gods on Mount Olympus. In her fury, Demeter causes the earth to become barren, until Zeus intercedes and works out a compromise whereby Persephone will spend only one-third of the year in the subterranean regions and two-thirds of the year with her mother on the verdant earth.

While it is traditional to see in this narrative the powerful ebb and flow of the agricultural cycle, feminist scholars see a celebration of the primal bond of mother and daughter. I see it as another version of the doubleness of women. Most of us are mothers and daughters too, and we are moved by different impulses in each of those roles.

Refuge, by Terry Tempest Williams, is an eloquent book about the cycles of the world of nature and the bonds of mother and daughter. Williams helps her fifty-eight-year-old mother through the passage of death by cancer, an inversion of the loss in the classic myth. Throughout this searing process, the daughter, a naturalist, also documents the ebbs and flows of the wildlife refuge at Great Salt Lake, Utah.

Last week, as I read *Refuge*, I brooded on the fact that I don't know that kind of fierce mother-daughter attachment—Demeter and Persephone, or Diane Tempest and Terry Tempest Williams—except what I read in books.

Double Woman. Emotionally, I am motherless. Perhaps it is for this reason that I am also daughterless, fearing the reproduction of hurtful patterns. I've been my own mother, self-reliant and mostly self-supporting since I was fourteen. And what stands in for my daughters? My scholarly works? My artistic ones?

Ruth, Aldona, and I are all daughters of difficult, disturbed women. Each one of us had a painful childhood and a traumatic adolescence. Each is from a family of daughters only. Ruth finds it significant that all of us have turned our backs on our mothers' sorts of lives, becoming scholars, intellectuals, and professors. Aldona and I have turned our back on motherhood as well. Ruth, in contrast, has successfully stopped the cycle of pain and neurosis that her mother inflicted on her and on her sister who committed suicide some years ago. She has two glorious teenaged girls, with whom she has a full and happy relationship.

The great nineteenth-century African-American quilter Harriet Powers called her famous Bible Quilt, now housed in the Smithsonian, "the darling offspring of my brain."[35]

In regard to *Dreaming of Double Woman*, what did I do when my offspring grew rebellious, when the work got difficult, painful, and bumpy? I cut off my relationship with my book. Cut it off cold. I had written or edited a number of books before this failure, so it was not simply the challenge of a big project. But this was the first one that was personally meaningful, about women's arts. Perhaps the first that I nurtured and cared for and to which I felt deeply and personally committed.

This week I've been thinking again about packing up the big old unwieldy manuscript and all its scholarly detritus. This impulse stems, in part, from a desire to make some order in a terribly disordered study; moreover, I want to make room for the new files, photos, and Xeroxes I've been accumulating during the Alaska research. Yesterday I bought the necessary cardboard file boxes at the office supply store. Now I need to work up to the act itself.

This has been a season of deaths: my work, my father, my bloodhound, even my car of fifteen years! I have this image that as I pack up the *Dreaming of Double Woman* manuscript and files I should do it in a ceremonial way. Wrap her in cloth for her interment.

A number of my quilt pieces or quilt tops wait patiently for the return of my attention. I do not mourn their lengthy gestation periods.

Finished portions, uncut yardage, and half-sewn scraps are folded away in boxes, awaiting my return.

Perhaps my book, that darling daughter of my brain, will only be shrouded in darkness for a few seasons more, undergoing some transformation that I do not yet fully understand.

JULY 1994

Sister's Choice

S ister's Choice is one of many blocks that can look completely different depending upon how color is placed and whether two, three, or four fabrics are used. A touch of bold color in each of the four corners allows the corner squares to push forward, while the pieces around them recede, making a three-dimensional object floating in space. When all four corner squares plus the light colored triangles that march around the edges are made of the same light-colored fabric, in alternation with one darker color, a flat, flowerlike pattern emerges around a central nine-patch. Like sisters, formed of the same genetic fabric, Sister's Choice squares are fashioned of the same pattern pieces, but very different-looking blocks result. A strong family resemblance remains.

Sister's Choice: I don't know what kind of memories are most typical for a little sister to have of a big sister. In my experience, they share the exhilaration of art making. B. J. left home for art school when I was just four years old, so my memories of her as a daily member of our household are very slight.

When I was five and six, I was allowed to visit B. J. at her apartment in Boston. From my adult vantage point, I marvel at the generosity of a busy art student who allowed her five-year-old sister to stay for an entire weekend. While ice cream cones, books, and rides on the swan boats in Boston Garden form part of my memories of those weekends, the most vivid recollections revolve around the making of art.

Clearly it is from B. J. that I internalized at an early age that women make art. And I learned to take the work of busy women seriously, be it sketching with charcoal, using yarn and needles, or sewing quilts.

When I visited B. J. while she studied at the Massachusetts College of Art, she bought me real artist's materials at the art supply store, not simplified nonstaining versions for children. I used Conte crayons, drew on real Arches paper, and learned of the messiness of charcoal and the remedy of charcoal fixative, all before I was seven.

The first and most vivid of these materials that I recall were what I termed the Magic Pencils. These looked like ordinary pencils, but when you dipped the points in water they skated across the drawing pad like watercolors. I used these throughout my childhood, and B. J. always refreshed my supply. I didn't know any other child who had them.

When I was ten, B. J. taught me how to use her sewing machine. The first lesson: with no thread in the machine, I was to take a lined piece of notebook paper (much like the kind upon which I am drafting this essay) and practice sewing in straight rows, following the pale blue lines. Next, the same but with thread, in order to practice threading the needle and breaking off the thread at the end of the row. I copied her example and slipped my sneaker off my right foot as I pressed the foot pedal. (She must have taught Judith the same thing, for even today all three of the Berlo sisters sit at the sewing machine unshod, for better contact with the foot pedal.) I soon graduated to working with real fabric. We picked out colorful cotton prints and a pattern for a straight shift. These were easy to sew and ever so stylish that summer of 1962.

B. J. was, and remains, an indifferent housekeeper and positively balks at the idea of cooking a meal. In this we differ, for I love to cook and revel in my domestic comforts. Apparently I learned these traits elsewhere. From my oldest sister I learned at an early age that making art is one of life's necessities, more vital than a hot meal or an orderly household.

Sister's Choice: from Judith I think I absorbed a sense of personal style. When I was ten and eleven she worked at Casual Corner, a woman's clothing store, in Boston. She brought home all sorts of marvelous outfits and wore them with such panache! From her I learned how to tie a scarf just so and the pivotal importance of the proper belt. Even today, if you are feeling chilly on a winter afternoon in Judith's Maine house and ask to borrow a sweater, she'll assess what you're wearing and bring you one that matches.

More recently, I continue to learn and be humbled by Judith's extreme sense of responsibility, patience, and generosity toward our parents. She made my father's last three months very happy ones, with her cheerful presence and her thermoses of soup, imported from Maine to Boston four times a week.

My career path has been very different from my sisters' in that I've not raised children but focused singlemindedly for almost twenty years on an academic life. It is only recently that the patterns of my life have come more closely to resemble theirs, as we all are enlivened by daily immersion in color, pattern, and piecework.

Sisters' choices can seem quite different, but there is an underlying pattern (be it of genetics, of intellectual proclivities, or of temperament) that unites them. Aldona and Ruth are the sisters of my adult life. It is a freely chosen sisterhood, based on affinity and intellect rather than consanguinity.

In 1981, with my heart in my throat, I gave my first talk on Native American art at a national conference. As an interloper from another field, I was nervous about this new territory. At the end of the afternoon, an important scholar, one whose many published articles I had read, approached me.

She stuck out her hand and said, "Hi, I'm Aldona. I wanted to meet you. I heard your brilliant talk this afternoon, and afterward I turned to Zena and said, 'Who is this person, and why don't we know her?'"

I thought I had died and gone to heaven.

Since then, our friendship has steadily blossomed. In its early years, she helped me through the rocky stages of leaving my first husband. Later I returned the favor. And through the years, a steady stream of phone calls: laughter and tears about jobs, conferences, lovers, colleagues, and all the other scraps of life.

Although Aldona and I have been friends longer, it is actually Ruth whom I have known the longest, though she didn't know me. I heard her give a talk at a conference in 1975. I was a first-year graduate student at Yale, she an advanced Ph.D. candidate at the University of London, recently returned from her fieldwork in Africa. She seemed staggeringly smart yet also very congenial and approachable. She was a role model for me, albeit a fleeting one: a tall, dark-haired woman, nearly done with her Ph.D., who had survived the crucial rite of passage known as fieldwork and come back to America to give an erudite lecture about it.

Ten years later, while conducting research in a Canadian museum, I saw Ruth again and, surprisingly, recognized her. (We six-feet-tall women remember others of our tribe.) She was deep in conversation with another museum curator as they installed an exhibit of Native American art. I was an established professor myself by then and, like Ruth, a recent convert to Native American studies.

Over the past few years, Ruth and I have shared work and confidences, coauthored articles, and told tales about our husbands. For both Aldona and me, she is very much the big sister. She assumes this role automatically, I think, because in her own family she was the big sister. Combining that with twenty years of motherhood, she is used to looking after all us girls.

Just as B. J., Judith, and I have our particular roles that we customarily enact, so do Aldona, Ruth, and I play off each other's quirks and patterns. Aldona is the one who is volatile, upsets easily, gets depressed. When this happens, Ruth and I, in turn, each start our own little spins. Ruth gets worried and protective; she sees her own little sister, the one she lost. She'll always be worried about losing another. I see what's inside me but doesn't manifest itself on the surface, the way it does with Aldona: all the anger, the insecurity, the longing for love.

I was nervous as the time approached for our third annual Female Scholars' Academic and Gourmandizing Retreat. At the first one, at Ruth's lakeside cottage in Ottawa, the manuscript of *Dreaming of Double Woman* was the main order of business. Last year, *A Wealth of Thought*, Aldona's book on anthropologist Franz Boas had center stage. This year, *Trading Identities*, Ruth's manuscript on Indian art made for the tourist market, is the main topic of our critique, but usually we each have something to offer for the group's critical attention: an article in progress, a grant proposal, a book outline.[36]

This year, I brought this manuscript in progress. I spent the last three weeks intensively editing and reformatting my computer disk in order to have one seamless manuscript with consecutive pagination rather than two dozen different files. I had spiral-bound the pages to signal to myself that it's almost finished, almost a book, a gift for my sisters.

Although it chronicles an intensely personal odyssey of the last two years, it is, at the same time, a book I hope to publish. As such, it needs shaping, more editing, and critical eyes other than my own. I sent pieces of this book to Ruth and Aldona over the past year, missives that conveyed more of my distress than anything else could. They are my perfect first audience for the initial 162 manuscript pages: tough but loving critics. They praise me lavishly, as dear friends should. They cry at the proper parts. They are firm about the excisions and changes that need to be made. They are confident that it will be published, and their assurance gives me confidence too.

Ruth's manuscript was, as she herself is, astonishingly smart and insightful. Beautifully written too. Aldona and I read it and shake our heads: "She's too smart for us. How can she stand to be friends with us? We'll never be this smart. Listen to this sentence!" Then one of us reads a weighty yet elegantly phrased line that offers some superb scholarly insight.

Sometimes we poke fun at the lofty tone, if only in self-defense. Aldona is lying on her bed reading Ruth's chapters, while I'm on the couch doing the same. Ruth is reading Quilting Lessons on the easy chair near me.

"Aldona!" I call out.

"Yes, ma'am?"

"See page fifty-seven, the middle of the page?"

"Yes?"

"Haven't you always felt, as the author so stunningly points out here, that 'essentialist discourse hates a hybrid'?"

"Oh, absolutely," Aldona agrees. "I was just saying that to my secretary the other day. 'Hazel,' I said, 'don't ever forget that essentialist discourse positively despises a hybrid.'"

We burst into peals of laughter. Ruth reddens and sinks into her chair. I make a mental note to immortalize this phrase on a pieced and embroidered pillow for her sometime soon—an arcane joke that only such pedantic sisters can share.

This year Aldona had no manuscript for us. At the end of a dizzying year as a new museum director, she has had no time for her own scholarly pursuits. But, sadly, she has brought a different order of business to the roundtable. I had been with her on Monday when her doctor performed a cervical biopsy because of highly irregular cells in her Pap smear. Ruth arrived on Wednesday night. Thursday morning Aldona was to get the results. We intended to go with her to the hospital, but she was adamant that she would go alone. End of discussion.

I understood. Sometimes when things are flying all to pieces I too can only hold them together if I keep others at arm's length, don't allow too much sympathy to reach me. Ruth and I waited at home, eating, chatting nervously, feeding biscuits to Annie, the sixteen-year-old yellow lab. We look out the window as each car passes, reassuring each other that the forty-five minutes, the hour, the seventy-five minutes didn't have to mean bad news.

When the car turns into the driveway two hours later, we know it is not good. The cell profiles presage cancer. A hysterectomy now is good news, though, for it almost guarantees that the cancer will be held at bay.

Aldona, brave as always, extorts promises of vast amounts of chocolate from us when she is recuperating. (I have sworn to her that a hysterectomy means that there is more room in the abdomen for chocolate treats.)

We will face this together, as we always do. That is the sisters' choice.

JULY 1994
Sedna, Squared

P eriodically, I haul out a portion of The Book, taking my academic pulse and temperature to determine if I can bear to work on it.

"It's like taking out quilt squares you worked on a few years ago," I try to reason with myself. "Maybe you'll complete it the way you initially planned, or maybe something else will take shape."

Since I'm on my way to Alaska for the second time this summer to conduct some research, I take out one section of the chapter on Inuit (Eskimo) women's arts.

"Just bring it along on the trip," I cajole. "Maybe you'll have a burst of inspiration in some hotel room."

Meekly, I obey.

In traditional Inuit religion, Sedna was the most widely revered and feared spirit in the north. Her image persists even in art made by the most contemporary and acculturated of Inuit artists. For the Inuit, as for us, myth lives on because it is a rich lode to mine as we seek pattern and order in our world. In an effort to tackle one small, nonthreatening part of the book, I decided to try to explore—to play with—the many stories of Sedna, to see if I could find a coherent pattern.

Rich in meaning and metaphor concerning female power, autonomy, and creativity, Sedna's stories are protean and differ from region to region. In some variants, Sedna marries a sea gull (or a man who later turns out to be a sea gull) who promises her fine animal pelts in her new home across the water. These promises are lies, for the sea gull lives in a wretched home with meager goods. Sedna's father comes to rescue her from this misery and takes her away in his boat. This angers the sea gull, who whips up a squall by beating his wings, so that the boat begins to founder. The father, caring more for his own life than for his daughter's, throws Sedna overboard in an effort to save himself. Sedna clutches at the sides of the boat, but her father cuts off her fingers, which transform into seals, walruses, and whales. Sedna sinks to the bottom of the sea, where she continues to create and control all sea animals.

I'm traveling in Anchorage and Fairbanks, conducting research on contemporary art of the Yup'ik and Inupiaq peoples (the two principal Alaskan Eskimo groups). At the Museum of the University of Alaska (Aldona's museum), I meet Susie Silook, an artist of Inupiaq and Siberian Yup'ik parentage. Her sculpture is on display, and she is at the museum to talk with museum visitors about her work. Her family comes from St. Lawrence Island, where men have been carving walrus ivory for centuries. She carves walrus ivory too, one of few women to do so. Her work is streamlined and contemporary. She intrigues me. I take her to lunch.

We talk about her being a carver, when most Alaskan Eskimo women make art out of sealskin, gut, and fur. She says she never was very good at sewing.

"Eskimo women have a phrase," she tells me, "for women who just don't have a clue about traditional women's work."

"Oh? What's that?" I ask.

" 'She doesn't even own a thimble,' they say in disgust. That's me. I don't even own a thimble." A wide grin splits her round face.

Her father was a hunter as well as a carver. Today, at age seventy, he still carves.

"He never said 'girls can't carve,' like some men. So I learned how to carve," Susie tells me, fingering her knife and fork as if she is assessing how she would carve them.

Her sculpture of Sedna, called "Seeking Her Forgiveness," is sleek and elegant, made from the whole, long length of the walrus tusk. About this work, Susie Silook says, "Native religions show respect for Sedna. When taboos were broken, Sedna's hair would tangle, and she wouldn't allow animals to be caught by the hunters. So then the shaman would have to journey underwater to placate her by combing her hair. This is like a prayer."[37]

I have brought my thick file folder of notes and photocopies concerning Sedna on this trip. The next night, in a hotel room in Anchorage, I reread the diverse myths, trying to unravel their dense, overlapping patterns.

I doubt that I will ever make a quilt composed of regular, repeating blocks. I prefer my serendipity method: start with a recognizable block such as a Star or a Four-Patch, then build haphazard abstract designs around it with scraps of cloth. There is no predictable, reassuring regularity, just increasingly complex asymmetrical designs. To find out where the designs should go, I lay my pieces out on the floor and add to them. Tonight, I find myself sitting on the hotel-room floor, arranging and rearranging different versions of the Sedna myth and a host of photocopies of Sedna imagery in Eskimo art.

Taking a break from this, I sit at the small table in front of the window and look out over the river. Though it's almost midnight, it's still light, and fishermen are casting their lines into the water, trying to catch salmon. From my suitcase, I take a plastic bag of small patchwork squares that B. J. gave me. They are composed of little triangles of contrasting colors that have already been machine-stitched and pressed flat. Now comes the tedious job of using a plastic ruler and rotary cutter to trim them to precise one-and-one-half-inch size. It's a good task to take on a trip: small and portable, and too tedious to spend much time on at home.

When I have traveled previously in the Arctic, I have seen Eskimo women do the same: take out a bit of beadwork or hide patchwork and labor on it while waiting in a tiny hamlet airport in the Northwest Territories or at the Alaska Native Hospital in Anchorage or in the lull between events at the World Eskimo Olympics in a hockey rink in Fairbanks. Carrying this little bag of cloth scraps provides me with an oasis of domesticity. It reminds me of my identity as a quilter when I am "at sea" in a strange city or overextended in my scholarly work. It reminds me I can make something beautiful out of almost nothing: out of the work of my fingertips and little odds and ends of fabric.

As I cut, I think about Sedna. In each of her many stories, she abandons the human community. She does something nonsensical, something no practical Eskimo woman would ever do: she refuses to marry, or worse, she marries a dog, and then turns her dog-children against their father. Or she impulsively elopes with a stranger who is not what he seems to be. Out of these acts that invert normal female behavioral codes, she is transformed into the one who has ultimate creative power: giver and withholder of all life.

A small detail in one story suggests that she is not as unlike other women as she seems, a detail that perhaps only a needlewoman would pay attention to. One day, it is said, Sedna was sitting by the shore and a man in a kayak came sailing up.

"Let the girl who does not want to be married come down here," he says.

"That must be me, I suppose," she said. Taking her sewing bag made from the membrane of a walrus's kidney, Sedna approached the kayak.

She may be fascinated by the stranger, and she may be ready for an amorous escapade, but she doesn't go anywhere without her sewing bag! After she has sailed away with him, he turns into a sea gull. In one version, he lures her with promises of fine sealskins and other animal pelts. Presumably, this is why she needs her sewing bag. Perhaps her greed for fine sewing material, rather than the mysterious stranger, is really the lure.

There is a land-based variant of Sedna too: the Caribou Mother, who generated animal life not from her fingers themselves but from something she has made with her hands and the contents of her sewing bag. She cut up her own fur leggings into small pieces, and each became a caribou. Inuit women in the Canadian arctic say that this is why caribou have fur that goes in different directions on different parts of their bodies, just as fur clothing does. (I relish the idea that nature's idiosyncrasies are explained by a metaphor having to do with the nap of fabric!)

Since the time of this creation, Caribou Mother, like Sedna, has controlled the release of animals for human use. And these powerful spirit women expect humans to observe a strict separation of the bounty of the land and of the sea. Just as a woman must never combine caribou meat and seal meat in the same cooking pot, so too must she avoid sewing skins on the shore of the fishing creeks when the salmon are running or making caribou-skin clothing during seal-hunting season. While the dark, relatively inactive days of an Arctic winter might seem the appropriate time to stay indoors and sew, there were strong taboos about overdoing sewing in this season. If women were to sew too much while camped out on the sea ice, all the seals would be withheld by Sedna and kept in her undersea snow hut.

I am feeling oppressed by my many deadlines. The modern woman's complaint: pushed in too many directions, too much to do, not enough time to do it, my patience and creativity stretched thin.

As Sedna is described in one Eskimo poem, I am feeling "snappish and savage."

I take notes on an exhibition catalog I am reviewing, *Inuit Women Artists*, which contains original writings by the nine women whose prints, drawings, and sculptures animate the book's pages. They write about their lives, their aspirations, their childhood sorrows: the loss of a mother when the artist was a small girl, the upheaval of being taken to a tuberculosis sanitarium in Manitoba for three years at age five, the loss of a husband, the scourge of alcoholism in northern communities.

My own responsibilities seem ludicrous when I read the words of Mayoreak Ashoona, who, more than most women of her generation, continues to live a traditional, hard, land-based existence. In a remote camp on Baffin Island, her daily round of activities includes fishing, cleaning, preparing skins, sewing, thawing meat, cooking, hunting, AND making art.

With characteristic Eskimo understatement, she comments, "What I have found is that if you have other things to take care of, it takes more time to do drawings, to draw them properly with a clear mind."[38]

I have been traveling too much, not sewing enough. Things have gotten out of balance. I need to feel my rotary cutter in my hand (my version of the Eskimo woman's *ulu*, or all-purpose utility knife, I think to myself with a smile), and cut some fabric strips. I need to placate my internal Sedna, who demands that mental disorder be untangled by the rhythm of working with cloth and cutter, pins and sewing machine.

Sedna's connection to sewing extends beyond the single instance of taking her sewing bag along when she went off adventuring. In the twentieth-century Canadian Arctic, Sedna is credited with giving a number of technological innovations to Inuit people, including the sewing machine. They say that when a man was out looking for driftwood, he came across Sedna, beached up on the shore. She said that if he pushed her out into the water, she would reward him.

"At dawn, I will place here a gramophone, a gun, and a sewing machine," she promised.

And so she did. Now northern women make beautiful parkas and wall hangings out of wool, felt, and other yard goods, with Sedna's laborsaving device of a sewing machine.

I picture a quilt called "Sedna Squared." It would perhaps be one of those kaleidoscope quilts, with the fabric cut into jewel-like forms. Long fingers and tangled skeins of hair would multiply in geometric variants. Dark greens, grays, and blues, the colors of algae, seaweed, rocks, and northern waters. A reminder of what we crave, Sedna and I, when we are feeling savage and snappish.

AUGUST 1994

What I'm Longing For

M y internal compass has spun 180 degrees since I started these essays a little more than a year ago. I write this final essay on a plane, flying above the Alaskan panhandle, on my return from the second of my two research trips to Alaska this summer. I began the manuscript last summer, in my living room, the cozy place to which I had retreated after feeling spooked at my writing desk for so long.

Though I haven't charted my recent scholarly successes in these pages, over the last few months I was awarded four grants, which will allow me to have the next two years off from teaching in order to study and write about Native American art. Had I won these grants a year ago, I would have been terrified—afraid that I couldn't resume the intensive scholarly pace that I had kept up for many years. It took a lot of quilting to get me to realize that I don't have to. I do it differently now.

The process of integration has begun. In small increments, I have laid out a pleasing pattern. I am confident that the next two years will be capacious enough to incorporate all of the pieces of me: quilting, writing personal essays, traveling to museums and Native communities, and writing scholarly studies.

Last night, eating caribou teriyaki and drinking a glass of Merlot, alone in a restaurant overlooking Cook Inlet, south of Anchorage, I made a list of the things I need to do in the next few weeks. It reflects the different parts of myself that were at war for so long:

complete a challenge quilt for the Louisville quilt show in late August

write a review of the Alaska Native art exhibit I saw in Anchorage

write the first of several articles that draw upon my research in the north this summer

finish this book of essays and try to get it published

finish an article on Northwest Coast button blankets that I owe *Piecework* magazine

My first task is to complete the quilt, for it must be postmarked by August 5. It is August 1 as I sit on the plane, flying above glaciers. The challenge quilt is based on incorporating half a yard of one designated fabric, a rich turquoise, purple, black, and blue paisley, into any design or pattern of my choosing. The top is already pieced, and the cutout, stuffed hearts and hands that will be loosely stitched to it in 3-D effect are nearly done.

The pattern I devised last winter, interlocking St. Andrew's crosses of turquoise and black, is based loosely on a large work of art done years ago by my friend and colleague Ken Anderson, painter and sculptor, and husband of Katie. His piece is a large painted canvas to which roughly snipped sheet-metal St. Andrew's crosses have been sewn. Though I haven't seen the piece in a decade, it lingers in my mind's eye, not vividly but as an impression of floating crosses. As I recall, his piece was based on a Navajo rug design. And so the unbroken chain of creativity and influence spirals on.

My wall hanging also comes out of my own experiments in cloth. I first made the little hands when I wrote "(Black) Pansies for My Mother." They are two layers of cloth, black on the topside and purple on the underside, with black felt sandwiched between. The layers are machine-stitched together around the edge in bright yellow thread, right side out, so that a rough, unfinished edge is left.

The crosses are made up of three-inch squares, five of them to each squat, equilateral cross. I first realized the design possibilities of simple three-inch squares when I made Kevin Eckstrom's Chocolate-Raspberry Quilt. They reverberate differently here.

That's the thing about quilt making. All those little geometric patterns, in endlessly changing manifestations.

It feels good to write this. I haven't written anything in three weeks. And I look forward to sewing tomorrow, having not sewn in nearly three weeks either. This summer I've been flexing other muscles, ones that had been atrophying too long. I am rediscovering the fun of research: the exhilaration of having xeroxed two dozen arcane articles at the Polar Research Library at the University of Alaska and looking forward to reading them; the sparks that fly when talking about ideas with newly met curators, artists, and scholars.

The past two days in Anchorage have been almost perfect ones—as happy as any I can remember in the last two years. I was not lonely or impatient in my solitude, but replete. Full of the previous few days spent in Fairbanks, in the company of my two best friends. Full of anticipation at seeing my two best guys, the two-legged one and the four-legged one, in St. Louis soon. And bursting with new ideas and new contacts.

Yesterday I interviewed two program directors at the Alaska State Arts Council. I revisited a museum exhibit I'm writing a review about. I made a return visit to the "Musk-Ox Co-op," an organization of Yup'ik Eskimo women who knit the fine hair of the musk oxen into beautiful scarves and hats for sale. I needed to take photos for an article I'm writing. Liz Spud, the short, round-faced Yup'ik woman who coordinates the co-op, greeted my appearance with a cheery "I remember you! You had that beautiful jacket on when you visited us last month!" I was wearing a kimono-style jacket purchased from a vendor in Paducah last April. (Being recognized in Alaska by an Eskimo woman I'm interviewing for a scholarly article, because of her admiration of the resist-dyed Indonesian fabric jacket I bought at a quilt show is surely evidence enough that I'm reintegrating the seemingly disparate parts of my life!)

Yesterday I met a marvelous Yup'ik man who runs a major program at the Alaska State Arts Council, even though he seems to be only in his midtwenties. We laughed and conversed animatedly, and I promised to send him some data helpful to his work, just as he had been helpful to mine. Vernon Chilmeraq was tremendously erudite and gentle, a graduate of the University of Alaska with a degree in comparative linguistics. Growing up in a remote village in western Alaska, he spoke both Yup'ik and English and studied two more Eskimo languages, Inupiaq and Greenlandic, in college. After our two-hour morning meeting in his office, I excused myself, had a quick lunch, went to my next appointment, and then hurried to the Anchorage Museum to attend an afternoon performance of an acclaimed Yup'ik dance troop. When the performers filed out, there was Vernon, first in line, wearing a finely worked skin parka and hat, beating a walrus-stomach drum. I sat in the front row. Vernon turned his head directly to me and nodded gravely, but with amusement in his eyes as well, as if to say, "Now you see me as I am—not just a white-shirted administrator in a government office, but a traditional drummer and singer as well. These are not dissonant roles—they constitute my identity. To know all of me, you have to see this too."

It was an epiphany for me. Too often, we are so utterly reductive in how we classify each other and how we present ourselves as well. Vernon Chilmeraq is not simply a civil servant in a shirt and tie. Nor is he stereotypically an "Eskimo," with whatever outdated image that word conjures up. He may be the only Yup'ik who speaks four languages and the only Alaskan arts administrator who plays a Yup'ik drum. He is clearly a complex, precious individual, unlike any other. He balances many components within himself.

So do I.

A scholar, a writer of many disparate texts, a quilter, a wife, a sister. These are all parts of my whole. I am learning to feel less grinding of the gears as I shift from one role to the next in the course of a day.

I scribble this in the last few empty pages of my research notebook, which is filled with notes from archival files and quotes from interviews with museum curators and Eskimo artists. My bag of Alaska Xeroxes holds not only a tall stack of articles and reports, but recipes copied from Aldona's cookbooks and the notes I made in response to Ruth's and Aldona's remarks about the first draft of Quilting Lessons.

As I worked on the Louisville quilt, I decided that its name was What I'm Longing For. It came to me, unbidden, just as Navajo Star Map had. Two hand patches, their pattern traced from my left hand (the one I write with), reach up from the lower left hand border of the wall hanging. One lone hand reaches down from the upper right. Hearts float in between. Other, more subtle hands and hearts form the machine quilting on the piece, competing quietly with the louder black and turquoise pieced crosses. With all those hearts and hands, and its title, it should be about love, I suppose. But for me it is about work. About longing to find integration and peace in my work—in the disparate products of my hands, all of which are, indeed, the "darling offspring of my brain," as Harriet Powers reminds me.

In What I'm Longing For, the tension and movement is produced by the fact that all of the crosses are pieced of squares of the same size fabric. As one's eye moves over the piece, sometimes the black crosses stand out, and then the turquoise ones do. Because each is composed of three or four different fabrics, their ad hoc, patchwork quality is emphasized.

Much unfinished work remains, both in the study and in the quilt studio. I sent two scholarly articles to their publishers before I left for Alaska; I'll send the wall hanging to Louisville by the due date.

What I'm Longing For is finally within my reach.

APRIL 2000
Postscript

I t is the spring of 2000 as I finish the final round of editing on Quilting Lessons. In the six years since I wrote the first tentative drafts of this manuscript, I did, in fact, finish writing three other academic books. During the last stages of each, I sometimes found myself working with the single-minded stamina and zealotry I had developed at the height of Quilt Madness, working for ten or twelve hours a day, not only because deadlines necessitated it, but also for the sheer love of the work.

Also within those six years, I embarked upon the most collaborative stage of my academic career. I received a grant from the Getty Foundation to work with Arthur Amiotte, a distinguished Lakota artist and scholar. In 1994 and 1995, we spent many weeks driving across the Great Plains, from Indian reservations to state historical societies to art museums, researching nineteenth-century Plains Indian drawings. (Like quilts, such drawings open a window onto a world of aesthetics, economics, religion, personal interrelationships, and individual biography.) During those long trips in Arthur's pickup truck, ribald pun making in Lakota and English alternated with serious discussions of traditional Lakota cosmology or contemporary artistic practice.

One day we began to talk about quilts. I told him about my descent into Quilt Madness and my meandering road back to academic work.

"I can't switch easily from art making to scholarship in one day," Arthur confided. "I'm better off if I involve myself totally in the visual world of the studio for three months, then take a break and write a bunch of lectures or papers."

To my surprise, Arthur was a quilt maker too.

"Oh, yes," he said airily. "You know me principally as a collage maker, but I've done everything from painting and drawing to weaving and quilt making. I've made traditional buckskin clothing for ceremony and adorned it with feathers and beadwork. My grandmother Christina taught me how to do all those women's arts—beadwork, quillwork, hide tanning. I enjoy all of it. Sometimes my aunties and I make quilts for give-away ceremonies and honoring ceremonies."

A man who had practiced every sort of art, as well as the most impeccable scholarship, clearly was an excellent role model and academic collaborator for me in the years directly after my quilting hegira. My work with Arthur, who became my good friend, was far different from any academic work I previously had pursued.

One time he suddenly drove off the main road and down a dirt road, having caught sight of a distant banner flapping in the wind. We pulled up at the recently deserted site of a Sun Dance ceremony.

Arthur bent down at the edge of the dirt track. "See these two different kinds of sage growing here? We use them both in cere-monies, for purification." He picked some and handed it to me.

I held the fragrant medicinal sprigs, warm from August sunshine, up to my nose. "Clean, astringent. They smell like they would purify you," I agreed.

We walked into the abandoned Sun Dance circle.

"In the ceremony, the young woman chosen to be White Buffalo Woman would come slowly, slowly, up over that ridge, huh?" He gestured to a slight rise at the edge of the circle.

"The people would recall how White Buffalo Woman brought many of the ceremonies and rules for daily life that Lakota people still follow. And see, up on the pole, all the cloth banners that people tie up? They blow in the wind. You can see them from far away, so you know where the ceremony is taking place. In the late nineteenth century, the Lakota became a cloth culture. Trade cloth became important to all aspects of our ceremonies and daily life. Stroud cloth, the heavy wool used for wearing blankets, and all those great calicos, ginghams, and plaids. We see the women wearing them in all the late nineteenth-century draw-ings we've been looking at. What a great new medium for art, huh?"

Arthur bent down again and picked up a flat rock. "I think you should have this stone from the pile that held the Sun Dance pole up, don't you?"

It sits on my worktable today, reminding me that scholarship is not a unidimensional, linear path, conducted exclusively in Ivy League research libraries.

Every day, in August of 1995, we would drive long distances over the flat roads of the Dakotas, examining and discussing color Xeroxes of some newly discovered Lakota drawings from 1880 that were going to be auctioned in New York that autumn. Arthur would gesture with his right hand, his left hand holding the wheel steady. I'd scribble notes as fast as our conversation flew, later staying up late into the night transcribing them into my laptop in my motel room.

In one drawing, a Lakota girl was sitting in front of a tipi, her face painted red for the ceremony marking the conclusion of her first menstrual period.[39]

"That's *Isnati Awicalowanpi*," Arthur said. "That means 'singing over the one dwelling alone.' She's in her first menstrual seclusion, huh?

"See that beautiful beaded dress she's wearing?" Arthur gesticulated with his pursed lips—a characteristically Lakota movement—toward the photocopy I held in my hand.

I nodded.

"At the end there's a gift-giving ceremony. She'll give that away to someone in the tribe who is poor, to instill the virtue of generosity."

"I've read in the old anthropology texts that the time of menstrual seclusion was considered a good time for making art," I offered.

"That's right. It's a woman's powerful time, when she's 'on her moon,' as we say. Outsiders have sometimes thought that women left the camp circle to go to the menstrual tipi because they're 'dirty,' huh? But that's not it at all. She's powerful then, and her power conflicts with other ceremonial powers in the community. If she devotes herself to making art then, she'll grow up to be industrious and artistic.

"Now check the map, Janet," Arthur continued, changing course. "And see how far we are from that Indian casino. We could get a good, cheap lunch there, huh? Before we go see the old ladies?"

Then we stopped for lunch and a side trip to the grocery store, where Arthur picked up a watermelon, a can of coffee, and other assorted groceries to bring as a gift to the "old ladies" we were going to drop in on that afternoon (Lakota noblesse oblige still being a highly valued cultural trait). These elderly Lakota women were artistic and ritual experts. To one of them, Darlene Young Bear, we showed the drawing of the young woman and the tipi we had been discussing in the morning.

"Almost nobody does this ceremony any more," she said. "They don't know how. We could use these pictures to help remember."

On some days, I would drive the pick-up, so Arthur could sit in the passenger seat and correct page proofs of a children's book about Plains Indians for which he was a consultant, or study some old Xeroxes from the Smithsonian he hadn't looked at in years but that might be useful for our work. And so, over the course of a summer, I learned again what I had begun to learn in my own "Quilting

Lessons"—that academic work, like quilting, can be done in bits and pieces: an hour in the pickup truck here, an hour on the motel patio there. I felt that I got my advanced degree in Native American studies in those summer sessions at the university of the prairie. Part of the curriculum was remembering always to make time to smell the sage or to bring groceries to the old ladies and talk with them quietly for a half hour. These acts of grace are fundamental to life's educational process too.

In 1995–96, I was project director for a major traveling exhibition of Plains Indian drawings. This was a vast patchwork of collaboration, as all major museum exhibits are, involving not only curators and scholars, but designers, editors, fund-raisers, Native consultants, philanthropic foundations, collectors, and the general public. I learned even more about letting go of the model of solitary scholarship. An exhibit is the academic equivalent of a quilting bee: it may have been my intellectual quilt everyone was stitching on, but I had to learn to sit back and relinquish control. We were all busily finishing up the project, so that it could be presented to the world in an exhibit and a fat illustrated catalog. We all shared the credit for this collective enterprise.

Having just finished another book, I have been thinking again recently about Arthur's comments about total immersion in art for a time, alternating with total immersion in the world of nonvisual ideas. Sometimes I love the feeling of surrendering completely to a project: when the embryonic quilt—or chapter—has such a compelling hold on my brain that I can't bear to be apart from it; when I look up, nearly mute, as if returning from a great mental distance, as Bradley arrives home at 6 P.M., wondering why there are no enticing dinner smells to greet him; when I wake up at 3 A.M. and lucidly scribble a note to myself or sketch a border design in the notebook by my bed, before ebbing back into sleep. But as with any great passion, this can't be the model for life every day. It is episodic. A gift when it comes.

In terms of daily life, I'm finally finding it most satisfying—and nearly automatic—to embrace a model in which a morning's work might, like today, include two hours at the writing table revising a manuscript, followed by an hour stitching the binding on the baby quilt I'm making for a friend, followed by an hour in which I put slides in order for the lectures I'm giving in three distant cities at the end of the month. Finally I clear my head by a half hour of chopping the vegetables for tonight's fragrant curry, wondering how that shade of persimmon in the squash I am slicing would look in the Autumn Leaves Quilt I am finishing for an invitational exhibit organized by my friend Kate Anderson.

Now *that* is a pleasing Serendipity Quilt of a day.

In 1997 I moved from St. Louis to western New York, to become the Susan B. Anthony Professor of Gender and Women's Studies at the University of Rochester. (As I nervously prepared for my job interview, I reminded myself that Susan B. Anthony gave her first speeches in support of women's suffrage at quilting bees. So perhaps it would be fitting for a quilter-scholar to serve as the Susan B. Anthony Professor at the hometown university that Anthony helped open to coeducation.)

The same week that I got word that the University of Nebraska Press might be interested in this manuscript, Judith and B. J. came for a visit. We sewed endlessly, of course, made the round of fabric stores, and discussed our mother. The usual stuff. After they left, I took out the last five Sisters' blocks that had been waiting patiently for me since 1993 and made another quilt.

Alas, *Dreaming of Double Woman* still lies dormant, in storage, along with a number of quilt projects. But I took it out this week to examine it in the light of some of the reviewers' queries about *Quilting Lessons* and found a manuscript much closer to completion than I had remembered. Perhaps it will clamor for my attention soon, and I will return to it with the joy and rapture with which I've embraced all these other endeavors.

Notes

1. Jonathan Holstein and John Finley, *Kentucky Quilts 1800–1900* (Louisville: Kentucky Quilt Project, 1982), plate 42.

2. Patricia Cooper and Norma Brady Buford, *The Quilters: Women and Domestic Art* (New York: Doubleday, 1977), 90.

3. Diane Bell, *Daughters of the Dreaming*. 2nd ed. (Minneapolis: University of Minnesota Press, 1993).

4. Patricia Cox Crews and Ronald C. Naigle, *Nebraska Quilts and Quiltmakers* (Lincoln: University of Nebraska Press, 1991), 108–9.

5. Crews and Naigle, *Nebraska Quilts*, 62–63.

6. Jacqueline M. Atkins and Phyllis A. Tepper, *New York Beauties: Quilts from the Empire State* (Dutton Studio Books and the Museum of American Folk Art, 1992), 130.

7. Judy Martin, *Ultimate Book of Quilt Block Patterns* (Denver: Crosley-Griffith Publishing, 1988), 19.

8. Melissa Meyer and Miriam Schapiro, "Waste Not, Want Not: An Inquiry into What Women Saved and Assembled: Femmage." *Heresies* 4 (1978):66–69.

9. Wendy Gilbert, *A Star for All Seasons Table Runner and Placemats* (San Marcos CA: A Quilt in a Day Publications, 1992).

10. Jean Wells, *The Milky Way Quilt* (Lafayette CA: C & T Publishing, 1992).

11. Judy Martin, *Scraps, Blocks, and Quilts* (Denver: Crosley-Griffiths Publishing, 1990), 55–71.

12. Margaret Miller, *Blockbuster Quilts* (Bothwell WA: That Patchwork Place, 1991), especially 82, 83.

13. This quilt, in the collection of the International Quilt Studies Center at the University of Nebraska, is illustrated in Jonathan Holstein and Carolyn Ducey, *Masterpiece Quilts from the James Collection* (Tokyo: N. Seto; Lincoln: University of Nebraska Press, 1998), plate 41.

14. As quoted by Pat Hickman, in *Innerskins/Outerskins: Gut and Fishskin* (San Francisco: San Francisco Craft and Folk Art Museum, 1987), 19. This book has splendid photos of traditional clothing and art objects made of fish skin.

15. Celia Y. Oliver, *Enduring Grace: Quilts from the Shelburn Museum Collection* (Lafayette CA: C & T Publishing, 1997), 93.

16. Diana McClun and Laura Nownes, *Quilts! Quilts! Quilts!* (Gualala CA: Quilt Digest Press, 1988), 104–5.

17. Atkins and Tepper, *New York Beauties*, plate 19.

18. Crews and Naigle, *Nebraska Quilts*, 212 and plate 95.

19. Cooper and Buford, *The Quilters*, 58.

20. See Maude Southwell Wahlman, *Signs and Symbols: African Images in African-American Quilts* (New York: Studio Books and the Museum of American Folk Art, 1993), figure 2.

21. "Crazy Work and Sane Work," *Harper's Bazar*, September 13, 1884.

22. These quilts and two tiny photos of her handmade clothing appear in *North Carolina Quilts*, edited by Ruth Haislip Roberson (Chapel Hill: University of North Carolina Press, 1988), figures 7.1–7.4.

23. See Wahlman, *Signs and Symbols*, figure 109.

24. Celia Y. Oliver, *Fifty-Five Famous Quilts from the Shelburn Museum* (New York: Dover Publications, 1990), 60.

25. *The New Quilt 2, Dairy Barn: Quilt National* (Newtown CT: Taunton Press, 1993), 75.

26. Crews and Naigle, *Nebraska Quilts*, 64.

27. Atkins and Tepper, *New York Beauties*, 75.

28. Brenda Peterson, *Living By Water*, (New York: Fawcett Columbine, 1990), xiv.

29. Published in *Double Wedding Ring Quilts: New Quilts from an Old Favorite*, ed. Victoria Faoro (Paducah KY: American Quilter's Society, 1994), 14.

30. Dean MacCannell, *The Tourist: A New Theory of the Leisure Class* (New York: Schocken Books, 1976), 13, 82.

31. Sue Bender, *Plains and Simple: A Woman's Journey to the Amish* (San Francisco: Harper and Row, 1989).

32. Dorothy Bond, *Blest Be the Quilt That Binds* (Eugene OR: Eugene Printers, 1992), unpaginated, Block #57.

33. Cooper and Buford, *The Quilters*, 94.

34. Janet C. Berlo, "Dreaming of Double Woman: The Ambivalent Role of the Female Artist in North American Indian Mythology," *American Indian Quarterly* 17, no. 1 (1993):31–43.

35. Gladys-Marie Fry, *Stitched from the Soul* (New York: Dutton Studio Books, 1990), 86.

36. I'd like to honor the work of my scholarly sisters by giving their books' full citations: Aldona Jonaitis, *A Wealth of Thought: Franz Boas on Native American Art* (Seattle: University of Washington Press, 1995) and Ruth Phillips, *Trading Identities: The Souvenir in Native North American Art from the Northeast, 1700–1900* (Seattle: University of Washington Press, 1998).

37. For illustrations of her work, see " The Sculpture of Susie Silook," in *Points North: The Arctic Circle*, a special issue of the literary journal, *Nimrod* 8, no. 2 (spring/summer 1995):28–29. See also in the same issue J. C. Berlo, " 'Great Woman Down There!' Northern Perspectives on Female Power and Creativity," 30–36, in which some of the same ideas in this chapter appear in a different format.

38. Odette Leroux, Marion Jackson, and Minnie Aodla Freeman, *Inuit Women Artists* (Vancouver: Douglas and McIntyre, 1994), 204.

39. Janet C. Berlo, *Spirit Beings and Sun Dancers: Black Hawk's Vision of the Lakota World* (New York: George Braziller, 2000), plate 19.

About the Author

Janet Catherine Berlo is an art historian, creative writer, and quilter. She teaches art history and women's studies at the University of Rochester in Rochester, New York. Her scholarly books include *Spirit Beings and Sun Dancers: Black Hawk's Vision of the Lakota World* (George Braziller, 2000), *Native North American Art* (with Ruth Phillips, Oxford University Press, 1998), *Plains Indian Drawings: Pages from a Visual History, 1865–1935* (Abrams, 1996), *The Early Years of Native American Art History* (University of Washington Press, 1992), and *Art and Ideology at Teotihuacan* (Dumbarton Oaks, 1993). She has received research grants from the Getty Foundation, the National Endowment for the Humanities, and the John Simon Guggenheim Memorial Foundation.

Berlo was a founding board member of the International Quilt Studies Center at the University of Nebraska, Lincoln (1998–2001). She lives in Greece, New York, with her husband, Bradley D. Gale, an industrial designer, and their Great Dane, Russell.